Fr Plot to Narrative

A STEP-BY-STEP PROCESS
OF STORY CREATION AND ENHANCEMENT

ELIZABETH ELLIS

PARKHURST
BROTHERS,
INC., PUBLISHERS

Parkhurst Brothers, Inc.
LITTLE ROCK

To Aisha —
Hope to hear
you tell soon.
Elizabeth Ellis

www.parkhurstbrothers.com

Parkhurst Brothers books are distributed to the trade through the Chicago Distribution Center, and may be ordered through Ingram Book Company, Baker & Taylor, Follett Library Resources and other book industry wholesalers. To order from Chicago's Chicago Distribution Center, phone 1-800-621-2736 or send a fax to 1-800-621-8476. Copies of this and other Parkhurst Brothers, Inc., Publishers titles are available to organizations and corporations for purchase in quantity by contacting Special Sales Department at our home office location, listed on our website. Manuscript submission guidelines for this publishing company are available at our website.

Printed in the United States of America

First Edition, 2012

2012 2013 2014 2015 2016 2017 2018
16 15 14 13 12 11 10 9 8 7 6 5 4 3 2 1

Library of Congress Cataloging-in-Publication Data

Ellis, Elizabeth, 1943-
 From plot to narrative : a step-by-step process of story creation and enhancement / Elizabeth Ellis. -- 1st ed.
    p. cm.
 Includes index.
 ISBN-13: 978-1-935166-81-8 (pbk.)
 ISBN-10: 1-935166-81-6 (pbk.)
 ISBN-13: 978-1-935166-82-5 (ebk.)
 ISBN-10: 1-935166-82-4 (ebk.)
 1. Narration (Rhetoric) 2. Storytelling. I. Title.
 PN212E55 2012
 808.036--dc23

                         2012005771

This book is printed on archival-quality paper that meets requirements of the American National Standard for Information Sciences, Permanence of Paper, Printed Library Materials, ANSI Z39.48-1984.

Cover and page design: Harvill Ross Studios Ltd.
Acquired for Parkhurst Brothers Inc., Publishers by: Ted Parkhurst
Editor: Barbara Paddack
Illustrator: Mr. Piecrust
092012

For Gene and Peggy
Connie and Toni

Acknowledgments

Many thanks to Susan Klein and Dr. Beck Weathers for their permission to quote from their work.

A special thanks to my family (all the generations of it).

To Ted Parkhurst for giving me this opportunity.

To David Ruthstrom and Allen Damron from whom I learned so much about making it work.

To Gail Rosen who first asked me to teach an intensive. To Kate Dudding, Meg Gilman, Jane Stenson, Ellouise Schottler, Jerry Falek, Jo Tyler and Robin Bady who followed suit. To all the tellers who have attended those weekends over the years. Much of this material came about because of each of you.

To Dr. Joseph Sobol and Delanna Reed for giving me a chance to teach in a more formal setting at East Tennessee State University.

To the folks at the International Storytelling Center, especially Susan O'Connor, and the folks at the National Storytelling Network, and the Timpanogos Storytelling Festival for your continued faith in me.

To the members of the Tejas Storytelling Association – Donna Ingham, Gary Patton, Jiaan Powers, Genie Hammel, Jeannine Pasini Beekman, MaryAnn Blue, Karen Morgan, Kim Lehman, Sheila Phillips, Finley Stewart, Tim Tingle and Doc Moore. You make me proud to live in Texas.

To Dr. Orvel Crowder, Cathy Crowley, Brooks Myers, Rayanna Talley, Betsy Bishop, Dan Keding, Loren Niemi and Gayle Ross. I couldn't have done it without you.

Contents

Introduction

This book is for the person who says,

"I have an anecdote, but I don't know how to turn it into a story."

And the person who says,

"I want to tell this piece from history, but I don't want it to be boring."

Or the person who says,

"I want to tell this story from the Bible, but I don't want them to fall asleep."

In short, it is for anyone who wants to create stories that are lively and meaningful.

In the last thirty years I have traveled the length and breadth of America (and some other places, too) telling stories and trying to help other people become more effective storywriters and tellers. I love to tell stories. In fact, I would rather tell stories than eat when I am hungry. But, the plain truth is that no matter how much pleasure I take from telling stories myself, nothing can compare with the joy of helping someone else become a stronger and more proficient story crafter.

Traveling around I get to hear a lot of less experienced tellers. I would sometimes think, "There is a good story there. Maybe even a great story. It's just waiting to be developed, that's all!" It is like bread that was taken out of the oven too soon. It never really had a chance to rise.

I bet you've found yourself in the same situation. You hear someone sharing their work and think, "Well, that was an interesting anecdote, but I wouldn't exactly call it a story. Surely a story has more meaning than that."

Or maybe you sat through a presentation of historical material, fighting to keep your eyes open while the speaker droned on until you found yourself not caring about what was being presented. You just wanted it to be over so you could go home and put on your pajamas, because sleeping in your bed is so much more comfortable than pretending not to be sleeping in a chair in a public place.

Or maybe you were seated in a pew when your head began to droop. And your last conscious thought before you descended into full-blown, head-back, mouth-open, humiliating snoring was, "The stories in this holy book couldn't possibly have started out this boring. If they had been, no one would have bothered to write them down." Zzzzzzzzzzzz.

I can see that I have struck a nerve. All of us have had these kinds of experiences. Our real fear is that we will be the presenter in one of these situations. I understand your concern. I have the same fears. Yes, really. I have spent a lot of time sharpening my skills in order to prevent my listeners from having that reaction. I feel I have developed some story building skills that could be useful to you and help you develop stories that are both meaningful and memorable.

I have talked to lots of people. Many of them were willing to share their story-crafting process with me. It often went something like this: sit at the computer and stare at the blank page for extended periods of time. Then, agonize over writing out the story word for word. Next, devote hours to memorizing what was written. Finally, get up in front of a group of people and try to share the story without having it sound as though it had been memorized.

What a lot of work! It makes my head hurt just to think about it. The thing that makes the pain worse is the realization that they don't get that much response after all that effort. It hardly seems fair.

Now, there is absolutely nothing wrong with writing down a story. I've been known to do it myself from time to time. The problem from my point of view is folks tend to begin in the middle of the process. They start by sitting down at the computer to write when they really aren't yet ready to do that yet. There is **a whole set of pre-writing exercises** they could do before attempting to capture the story on paper that would lay a strong and effective foundation for a more engaging story.

A few years back I read a quote at the bottom of an email from a friend. It said,

"The term 'narrative' is often confused with the term 'plot,' but they're not the same thing. If I tell you that the king died, and then the queen died, that's not narrative; that's plot. But, if I tell you that the king died and then the queen died of a broken heart, that's narrative."

I was really struck by the quote. I kept thinking of it over and over. It was attributed to Vladimir Nabokov. I just couldn't get it out of my mind. What if I could develop a process for helping folks move from the basic plot to meaningful narrative?

I began to think about my own process for story crafting. I could easily identify all the aspects of story that I examine when creating a tale or crafting one for telling. I started to create exercises that would be helpful in developing a deeper level of story making. I wanted to see if the process was useful for people. Workshops seemed the obvious way to test drive the material.

I used the quote that had started my thinking about this process, how to get from plot to narrative. As soon as I shared that quote with the group, one of the participants said, "Oh, that's a famous quote from E.M. Forster."

E.M. Forster? My friend had attributed it to Nabokov! In my search to find the true source of the quote, not only did I find it wasn't from Nabokov, I discovered it wasn't quoted correctly either. Life sure is a funny old dog!

It turns out what Forster really said is,

"Let us define plot. We have defined story as a narrative of events arranged in their time sequence. A plot is also a narrative of events, the emphasis falling on causality. 'The king died, and then the queen died' is a story. 'The king died and then the queen died of grief' is a plot."

I read the real quote from Forster several times, but what he actually said did not work for me the way the original misquote did. I found myself waking up in the middle of the night, realizing I had been dreaming about how to move from plot to narrative.

While researching the original quote, I found the misquote used in many places. I have come to believe that those who work with story needed a quote of this nature. I think the quote was so well known and so often quoted, it entered into the folk process. Every writer or storyteller who quoted it changed it to fit their own needs and beliefs. Perhaps what they developed worked better than the original quote. By now it is Internet Apocrypha.

I stopped caring about who said what or how accurate the quote might be. I decided to continue working on developing experiences that could help those who work with story move through the layers to get from simple plot to compelling narrative.

So my definitions for this book are simple and direct.

"Plot" is what happens in the story.

"Narrative" includes all the elements that make the story matter to us.

Working on this has been a big help to me. It forced me to think critically about my own process for story crafting. It enabled me to put into words some things I have always done intuitively.

But, you don't really care what I have learned from it. You want to know what it will do for you, right?

There are a lot of books about story creation and story crafting. Many of them are outstanding; they plumb every nuance of the story crafter's art. Those books are helpful if you already know what you are doing. If you don't, they can be overwhelming.

I wanted something easy to understand and easier to apply. I wanted something lighthearted, practical and down to earth. Most of all, I wanted something anyone could use and begin immediately to see a profound effect on their stories.

This is that book.

This book teaches a process. If you take the plot of a story and follow the exercises as they are given, you will develop a more appealing and compelling story. Honest.

The best part is that the process can be applied to any story:

- personal story
- family story
- folktale

- tall tale
- sacred story
- historical story

I could just as easily have listed:

- novel
- memoir
- film
- non-fiction presentation
- sermon
- trial

This process works well with every type of story on which you will ever want to work. Learning the process will be time well spent. Once you master it, you will see the results in your work.

Also, we tend to do the things we think we do well, and ignore what we know we don't do well. This is a pretty comprehensive process. Using it will keep you from doing a lot of work on the aspects of story with which you feel comfortable and ignoring those in which you don't feel you are as strong. The exercises are practical, and will give you a chance to grow your strengths in some new areas. You'll be a better story crafter for working with all the exercises, even the ones you find difficult.

Remember, there's nothing wrong with writing down a story. Just don't be in such a big hurry to get to that step in the process.

Elizabeth Ellis
Dallas, 2012

Laying the Foundation

Plot is a word folks seem to use a lot, but for which no one has an exact definition. For the purpose of working with this book, we are defining plot as the sequential events in a story. It is the basic "what happened" of any story. It is the skeleton on which the body of the story hangs. Like a human skeleton, it gives form and the possibility of movement.

Narrative, on the other hand, is more about the "why" than the "what happened."
Narrative is the way in which the plot is presented. It encompasses all those additional elements that make it possible to have an effect on the listener or reader.

The material in this book lays out a comprehensive process for beginning with a basic plot and examining the individual layers needed to turn that basic plot into meaningful and elegant narrative. There are ten layers offered for you to consider. If you will take the time to read about each layer and do the exercises that are suggested, you will find that it will make a profound difference in the quality of your story making.

This process works with any story – the kind of story doesn't matter. Considering each of these narrative layers will make for deeper and more involving stories to share. It may seem strange or time-consuming at first. By working this process, soon it will become second nature to you. I believe it will pay big dividends.

I grew up in the Appalachian Mountains. In that region, if you are telling about something that happened to one of your ancestors, you might say, "Somewhere back in the greats...." It means that you do not know how many generations back. It's a very useful expression, because it keeps you from having to say "my great-great-great-great-grandfather" each time you refer to him. Because you said, "Somewhere back in the greats," you can now just say "my grandfather." Your listener knows that you mean several generations back, and you are relieved of the clumsiness of having to say all those "greats" each time you speak about him.

This is a book that will be useful to storytellers and writers and filmmakers and poets and songwriters and everyone else who works with story in any way. When I first began writing, I was using a lot of those titles in nearly every paragraph. It was both time-consuming and clumsy. One day I started thinking about the expression, "Somewhere back in the greats…." It occurred to me that what I needed was an easier way to write about all those people who work with story without having to name them all.

So I invented a word: "storyer." I use it to mean all those folks who work in story no matter what form that may take. The more I used it, the more I liked it. I liked it because it made for smoother writing. Even more, I liked it because it acknowledges the common nature of our work. We all have much in common. I am glad to focus on that, instead of the things that separate us. In our culture, whenever we are speaking of a person who works in the arts, when we run out of superlatives to describe them, we always call them "a storyteller." Deep within, we remember that story is at the heart and unites us all.

Having decided to invent one word, it seemed a shame to stop there. Throughout this book I also use the word "storying" as a verb to describe the process of reading, listening, watching, or any other form of receiving a story. Just like "storyer," it makes for simpler and smoother writing and acknowledges the commonality of our work.

Although I did not invent the word "participant," I use it often to refer to the person who is listening, reading, watching or receiving our story making in some way. I chose to use that word to remind us that all those people are co-creators with us in our work. Without them, our work is useless. If they are not involved enough to be participating emotionally in the experience of the story, our work has no meaning. We all need to be reminded of that continually.

Picturing the Plot

All artists need materials in order to do their work. Story crafting of all kinds is an art form. If you work in story in any way, you too are an artist. You probably have your own process for working on a story. I hope you will suspend judgment for a while and work this process to see if it may be useful to you.

To work the process of story crafting put forward in this book, there are a few materials you are going to need:

- several sheets of plain, unruled paper
- a set of thin-line, colored markers
- a package of stick-on flags
- timer
- some gallon-size, zip-lock bags
- a pair of scissors

Right away I know that some of you have questions. That's the way we are! No, it doesn't matter what color paper you use. White and cheap are my favorites. Thin-line markers because the fat ones are good for making signs, but hard to draw with. Crayons or colored pencils will work, but we want the brightest colors possible.

Stick-on flags? Yep, you know those pre-gummed indicators that they stick on documents to indicate where you are to sign your name? The ones you use on the textbooks you are planning on selling back to the university? Those are the ones I mean. If you don't have them, you could cut some post-it notes in half and use those.

A timer? No need to run out and buy a stopwatch. The timer in the kitchen will do just fine. You can use your watch, but it's good to have a bell to ring to tell you when the time is up. Hey, maybe your watch does that. Check.

The gallon-size, zip-lock bags? They're for keeping your storyboards so you won't lose anything in case some of the stick-on flags come off. You may not have time to do all the work on your story in one sitting. In fact, I'd be surprised if you did. So stash the storyboards in the zip-lock bags until you have time to come back and complete your work on the story.

Scissors? What can I say? You're gonna have to look for them.

Now that you have all your materials assembled, let's get down to business.

I imagine that you already know **the human brain is divided into two halves.**

The left side of your brain deals in factual information. That's the part of your brain that knows what nine times nine is … if you know what nine times nine is. It is the side of your brain that knows your address, and how to figure up what to tip the waiter. It responds to facts, outlines, and charts. It understands language.

The right side of your brain deals in intuition and creativity. That's the part of your brain that imagines, conceives and invents. It responds to images and bright colors. It does not have language.

The problem with sitting down at the computer to write out your story word for word at the beginning of the process is that you are bypassing your greatest strength for the work. You would be working primarily out of your left brain. You would not be getting the best access to your creativity with this method.

Let's begin the process by making a **storyboard**. Nearly every film you've ever watched has been developed from a storyboard. It looks like the Sunday comic strips or a graphic novel. There is one picture for each scene in the story. **The pictures tell the plot.** This happened. Then this happened. Then this happened, so they could live happily ever after. No matter how long or complicated a story may be, it can be divided into scenes.

Remember I said several pages of unruled paper? You want to **put each picture on a separate page.** Why?

- you don't yet know the order in which the scenes go
- you don't want to have to redo the entire storyboard if you make a mistake
- you don't want to have to start over if you decide to add something

I know that some of you are drawing back about this time. I can hear you saying things like, "I don't know how to draw."

- no one is going to see this but you, unless you choose differently
- stick figures are fine
- all that matters is if you know what you mean by the picture you draw
- simple images work

No one ever displayed my drawings on the wall in grade school. I am not a visual artist. I believe that I am an artist. But, I am not a visual artist. I make pictures with words. If I draw a key on one of the pages, this image reminds me of the entire scene about when I locked myself out of the car on the day of my mother's funeral.

Give it a try. "I don't know what to put on the paper."

- picture one might tell us who the story is about – the main character
- picture two could tell us the problem or the conflict
- picture three might tell us the complications or how things got worse
- picture four could tell us the solutions that were attempted or how help arrived
- picture five could tell us how the problem was solved or the conflict was resolved
- picture six might tell us why it was important or why you choose to tell us about it

STORYBOARD:

MAIN CHARACTER	CONFLICT	THINGS GET WORSE
TRIALS	RESOLUTION	WHY

What I have listed above is a prototype only. I don't know your story or the form that it will take. Your storyboards may take a different shape. What you will put on your storyboards and how many pictures you will need are decisions you will make depending on the story. What I have listed is only for suggestion.

Remember I said the right brain works with images and responds to bright colors? Perhaps you are beginning to see why the storyboards are useful to us. We are making a **visual outline** of the story **for the creative side of our brain**. We are accessing its strengths for our work.

When I am **working on a long story**, I find it useful to do a storyboard for the overall story. I also make storyboards for each of the smaller pieces that are a part of the narrative. When I settle on the way I wish to share the story, I may consolidate all these pages into smaller drawings. But, I always begin with separate pages for each scene to give myself freedom to change my mind about the order – what to put in and what to leave out.

Making the storyboards is essential to the process we will be working. Each layer of the narrative we will be considering ends in a **practical exercise**. Every one of them sends you back to do additional work on your storyboards in order to enrich your narrative.

So stop stalling and make your storyboards.

Context

Tip: No need to begin a story with,
"Before I begin my story I need to tell you that . . ."
Any needed information can be
built into the body of the story itself.

"The noblest pleasure is the joy of understanding."
– Leonardo da Vinci

One of the first things we want to ask is, "What does the listener need to know in order to be fully engaged in this story?" You will want to give some thought to what information your listener needs in order to understand what is happening or why it is important. We have all been in situations where we felt like outsiders because we didn't know important elements about what was being presented. And what was our response? Usually we spent more time thinking about what we didn't know than what was being presented. Often it took us completely out of the story. We worried the unknown details like a terrier with a bone.

Sometimes the needed information is simple and can be handled with:

> "When I was a child in Cleveland . . ."
>   or
> "My grandfather's hardware store was the scene of much of my childhood."

These statements give context that gives us a setting, an idea of where the story is taking place.

Sometimes we need a sense of time in order to understand.

> "I remember being in the third grade. It sticks out in my mind, because…."
>
> or
>
> "The year my wife and I were married, John Kennedy was in the White House."
>
> or
>
> "Long before Columbus failed to discover a trade route to India…."

These openings set us in time, but they have the added bonus of creating in us a desire to hear more, to be curious about what will happen next.

There might be unusual words or phrases in the story. Context means giving your listener an understanding of what they mean.

> "I picked up my scythe, that long sharp blade I used for cutting hay, and…."
>
> or
>
> "He came out carrying a calabash, a large dried gourd for storing things."

Don't assume the participants know everything you know. I grew up on a farm. But I have discovered that the names and uses of basic farming implements are not known to those raised in the city. They know the word tractor, but if there is a harrow or a drag sled in the story, you might as well be speaking Greek if you don't build in some definitions for them. The younger your listeners, the less life experience they have under their belts and the greater the need for helping them understand what is happening in the story. At Christmas every year, I build into my story a definition of the word inn for the little ones. I don't assume they know what it means.

How far is a furlong? How fast is a knot? Stewing about these things can take your listener right out of the story. Hold them in the tale by giving them needed information in an artistic manner. It can be done smoothly with only a little practice.

The need for context may be more than giving the simple definition of a word.

If you are telling a family story, they may need to know something about the relationships of the people involved. Or perhaps about the family's structure or heritage.

A story I tell about my aunt and my mother has much more meaning for my listeners if they understand that for more than twenty years the two of them were next-door neighbors, but they did not speak. Not a word.

Dan Keding (www.dankeding.com) gives us funny and moving stories from his complicated childhood with adroit use of context. He helps you maneuver through Catholic school, the South Side of Chicago, and a Croatian grandmother without getting lost.

In a folktale there may be customs that are unknown or misunderstood. The tale will mean much more if your listener knows that arranged marriage is the acceptable norm for this culture. There will be a special significance to knowing that the bride wants to speak privately to the man she is arranged to marry. The need for absolute secrecy not only adds to our understanding, it adds to the suspense, as well.

A story from historical sources may require a great deal of context before your listeners are comfortable with the story. They may need to know far more than can be shared with just a simple definition of a word. Informing their listening is an important part of the storyer's art. The historical works of storyteller Judith Black (www.storiesalive.com) are an excellent example.

The same is true of stories from the Bible or other sacred text. Our understanding of the story and its meaning can only be enhanced by knowing the customs of the times and the places from which these stories come.

It is not enough to give people the needed information. We want to share it with them in an artistic manner that does not seem clumsy or interrupt the flow of the story.

Some useful techniques for sharing context are:

- dialog
- flashback
- letters
- newspapers
- diaries or journals

Dialog. It is far more interesting to hear two characters in a story talking to one another than it is to receive a lecture full of abstract facts. The same factual information can be absorbed by the listener easily if it is presented in an entertaining form. It is natural that an older person in the family would be giving information to a younger one. A local would have a lot that they could tell a newcomer. An old hand could be informing a new employee. Each of these scenarios would allow for sharing lots of needed factual information.

A few years ago I was asked by a local science museum to present a program to accompany a large robotic whale exhibit. They wanted the family audience to come away with a picture of what life was like when whaling was an important part of the American economy. I did some research and discovered it would be challenging to help others see how different life was

ELIZABETH ELLIS | 27

in the whaling villages because they were so much like things
are all over the United States today. Because the whaling villages
had been founded by Quakers, men and women were treated as
equals. Most of the businesses were woman owned and run. At
a time when African-Americans in the rest of the country were
being held in bondage, Quakers treated them as equals. There
were black ship captains and businessmen.

To help the listeners understand the whaling industry, I created
a young man who was going out on his first whaling voyage. All
the information about hunting for whales in the 1700s was given
to the listeners in dialog between the first mate and our hero
who was new to the ship and asking lots of questions. It was an
effective way to inform them.

Later in the story the young man, older now, marries and brings
his bride from the South to live in Nantucket. Through her eyes
the listeners got to see the sharp contrast between life in the rest
of the United States and in the whaling villages. As the newcomer
from a "different culture," she had lots of opportunity to comment
about the differences between her old home and the new place she
had come to live.

Flashback. We want the listener to enter the story at an interesting
and compelling moment in the tale. We want to catch their
attention and hold it. The flashback gives us the opportunity to
fill in any missing information from the past. It may answer the
question,

"What happened before this?"
or
"How did we get in this situation?"

If you think about it for a moment, I imagine you have seen
this technique used in many novels and films. Robert Ludlum

uses this technique effectively in *The Bourne Identity*, as Jason is regaining his memory. I tell several stories where the importance of what is happening in my adult life is given by flashbacks into my childhood.

Letters. Using letters can be an effective way to share needed factual information with your listeners. They might be historical letters from real people, such as using the letters between John and Abigail Adams to inform us about the writing of the Declaration of Independence. However, they could also be letters invented to fit the needs of the participants of the story. You might read from a letter that explains the importance of a discovery or an invention to give needed context for understanding the consequence of the event.

One of the big advantages to this method is you can "read" the letters to your audience. Of course, you will want to know the content very well so that you do not have to lose significant eye contact with your listeners while sharing it with them. But, using this method can make it possible to have a lot of dates or numbers readily available to share with your listeners without having to memorize all those facts.

An example of this epistolary style is seen in the novel *Fair and Tender Ladies* by Lee Smith. The author has set it in Appalachia and makes great use of letters both to give context and to develop the character of Ivy Roe, a most memorable young woman.

Jon Spelman (www.jonspelman.com), a storyteller from the Washington, D.C., area, has a very moving storytelling program called "War Stories: Nam." In it he makes effective use of reading pieces of letters from soldiers to the participants. Not only does it bring these men to life for us, it allows for the sharing of actual information about the war in a way that is artistic and impactful.

Newspapers. You can employ the same technique using newspapers instead of letters. Like the use of letters, what you share can be historical or imaginary.

Lucinda Flodin and her late husband, Dennis Fredrick – called the Story Weavers – used this technique successfully in their story about how women won the right to vote. Dennis would pretend to read to his wife from the newspaper, thereby giving details of the history of the struggle for women's suffrage. The listeners also got a wonderful view of the two main characters in the story by hearing their interaction at the breakfast table over the newspaper.

Diaries or Journals. This can be very useful in establishing the involvement of the character in the story in events of the time you wish to tell about. It can also be a way of showing the private thoughts of a character, a way to share doubts or feelings with the listener. Some selections from your father's journal during World War II can give needed information, but can have the extra advantage of letting us know how your father felt about it. By sharing from a diary or journal you kept at some point in your life, you can give us background information, but you can also show us what kind of person you were at that time in your life.

"Silver Spurs" is a powerful story Beth Horner (www.bethhorner. com) has developed from a Civil War diary kept by her great-great-grandfather.

Exercise. Look at the pictures in the storyboard that you have made of the plot of your story. Think about each picture in turn. What does your listener need to know to fully understand the story? There may be several places where you find your listener will need context in order to be fully engaged in the story. Some of them may be small pieces of information that can be handled quickly. Others may require much more. On your storyboard, mark each of these spots in the story with a stick-on flag. This will alert you to the need for providing context at this point in the story. As you develop your story, you may use some of the techniques that have been suggested. Or you may come up with a method uniquely your own. The important thing to remember is to give the needed information in a way that does not interfere with the natural flow of the story.

Conflict

**Tip: If there isn't any
conflict,
there isn't much of a story.**

*"The greatest conflicts are not between two people
but between one person and himself."*
– Garth Brooks

The chief problem with most anecdotes and many stories that seem dull to us is that they have **no conflict in them**. If you put the heart monitor on the story, it would **flatline**. As you are working through your story, try to remember that image. You want some life in your story. You want energy. If there is no heightening of energy or emotion in the story, there is not much to which your participants can respond. Considering the conflict in your story is the way to bring it to life.

As soon as the word conflict is mentioned, some people get nervous. They like to avoid conflict. It makes them uncomfortable. Conflict, however, is an inescapable part of life. Even those who choose to become monks cannot escape it. I am sure that it arises over how the potatoes are peeled or whether it is time to paint the interior of the monastery.

Conflict can be:

- small
- huge

Conflict can be small, like an argument between roommates over whose turn it is to load the dishwasher. It can also be huge, like a war between two countries that leads to much tragedy and suffering. Big conflict is easy to write about. All you need are two opposing forces that are going to do battle. You know that is easy to create because you see so much of that on television and in the movies. Small conflicts are entertaining to write about, too. They are often funny, and they may deal with experiences that the listener or the reader can easily relate to.

Make two fists. Put them together and push. Push hard. This is a good way to understand what is meant by conflict. It is two forces pushing against one another. Neither force will give in; each force wants its way. I use this technique when I am working on stories. As I examine the pictures in my storyboard, doing this as I look at each picture helps me identify where the conflicts in the story may be. It also helps me identify potential conflict of which I have been unaware.

Besides large and small, there are two kinds of conflict.

- external
- internal

External conflict is the conflict between two people. It is the battle between two forces. It is the Axis vs. the Allies. It is Star Wars. It could also be the ongoing battle between you and your baby brother, or the war between you and the medical establishment. Whether it is large or small, it is between two outer forces. It can be observed and recorded, although it is probably safe to say that each side of the conflict would tell it differently. In a story I tell about a wedding, the two conflicting forces are the mother of the bride and the mother of the groom. Believe me, each of them would tell the story of that conflict differently.

Internal conflict is conflict between the character in the story and their values. It is the war between our fears and who we truly want to be. It is the conflict you felt as a child between wanting to tell the truth about what happened and being afraid of getting in trouble. It is Edgar Allen Poe's "The Tell-Tale Heart." It is Jacob wresting with his angel. This is a story the "Sandwich Generation" knows very well as they struggle to strike a balance between their responsibilities to their aging parents and their still-needing-them children. I have more than one story about my fear that my responsibility for the grandson I raised would seriously affect the needs of my elderly mother and trying to resolve that dilemma. There is much to admire in the work of Jay O'Callahan (www. ocallahan.com), but I have always been impressed with his ability to share with us the internal conflict of his characters.

Internal conflict cannot be observed. It is secret. Cheesy cartoons on television show it to us in an observable way with the little devil sitting on someone's shoulder whispering into their ear, and the little angel on the other side, demanding equal time. That is so common, it has become a cultural icon. Everyone recognizes it instantly. For some stories it may be just the technique you want to employ. It lends itself to comedy really well.

But, some stories may require a **subtler approach:**

- **conversation with character's inner self**

- **imagined conversation with a mentor or hero**

- **imagined conversation with a deceased loved one**

- **role-played conversation with an authority figure or some other oppositional person**

- **going to a physical place that represents conscience**

Don't tell us the entire conflict in one chunk. Whether the conflict is internal or external, you will want to **build it in small steps**, like going up a staircase. This is a far more interesting way to build the tension in the story. In a story from my childhood, I tell about pushing my new bicycle through a nest of yellow jackets. I don't say, "They came out and stung me all over." That is certainly what happened. I remember it vividly, believe me. Instead, I say,

"I looked down and there was a yellow-and-black-striped bug on the back of my hand. I slung it off. It came right back. I was worried that it was going to sting me. I looked down and there were two of them on my hand. Then I noticed one on my other arm."

I build the tension in the story by giving it in small but increasingly more serious increments, until they are all over me. Part of the tension of the story is anticipating being stung for the first time. After that, the tension is in getting away from the yellow jackets altogether. I take my time in developing the participants' agony in watching this unfold in their imagination.

The external conflict in this story is between me and the yellow jackets. There is internal conflict, as well. It is my "only new bike you're ever gonna have in your whole life" bicycle. My mother has impressed upon me that I should never go off and leave it. There is great conflict going on within me between my desire to get away from a dangerous situation and my belief that I have to get home with the bike even though pushing it uphill is slowing me down.

If you are working with historical story, the external conflict may be obvious. It is likely to be about two opposing factions. Or about our struggle with the elements. You will have a much more compelling story if you look for the internal conflict as well. Robert E. Lee was the head of West Point when the Civil

War began. It was a struggle for him to decide where his deepest allegiance lay. He had trained many of the men who would lead the Union; they were his personal friends. His decision was made when he came to the conclusion that Virginia was his mother, and no man should take up arms against his mother.

The stories of going West are an important part of American history. Many of them would be more compelling if they included the conflict of the women involved who did not want to leave their families behind. Remember, a woman had no legal right to live separately from her husband. If he were going West, she was going, too. It was the law.

Stories from the Bible are often straightforward in the narrative that is given to us. The factual information is given about what happened. A richer story may be found in the why, or in the struggles of the character to do what is asked of them. We are given an account of Jesus standing in the doorway of the cave and calling, "Lazarus, come forth!" That is a powerful story. But, there is nothing in the text that tells us how long it took Lazarus to respond or what he was thinking between coming back to life and coming out of the cave.

Perhaps he was reluctant to leave a realm of bliss to return to this earthly existence. Perhaps he had to struggle with whether or not he was willing to return to a world of pain and hunger and hatred. Maybe he had to weigh the merits of this existence before he was willing to make the decision to come back to life. We don't know. But there is a compelling story there to be shaped. There is even a funny one, if you want to shape it that way.

If you want to introduce humor into your story, the internal dialogue of the characters may be a place to look. There is often fun in the great gulf between what we say to others and what we are saying to ourselves. Stress is what happens when your mind says, "Are you out of your mind to ask me to do something like that?" while your lips are saying, "Why I'd love to."

Exercise. Go back to your storyboard. Examine each frame of it in turn. Look for the places where there is external conflict. Now look for the places where there is internal conflict.

Mark each of these with a flag. On the flag write an **E** or an **I**, for whether the conflict is **External** or **Internal**. Ask yourself, "Is this conflict something I want to include in the telling of my story? If so, how will I tell it in the most artistic and intriguing manner?"

Sensory Imagery

**TIP: Remembering the story
will be much easier for you if you
imagine yourself walking around
in each scene of the story, observing sensory details.**

*"I want all my senses engaged.
Let me absorb the world's variety and uniqueness."
– Maya Angelou*

No matter how it is delivered, a well-developed story activates our imagination. When we are fully engrossed in story, we can see the events unfolding in our mind. As storyers, we want the participants to be so involved in the story that they feel as if they are present as the story is unfolding.

Look for a moment at these words:

- imagination
- image
- magic

You can see that all three come from the same root word and are related. When we help others use their imagination, they make an image, and something magic happens.

They are transported to a different realm. No matter how long ago or far away the story may be set, for this moment it is happening here and now in the active imagination of the participant. Sounds like magic, doesn't it? That's why we say things like, "She cast a spell over her listeners." Or, "The author's work held me enthralled."

Fortunately, you do not have to attend wizard school to be able to work such magic. You already have the ingredients for such a spell at your command. It is in the five senses of your reader or your listener. **Activate their five senses**, and you will be able to draw them deeply into the story. That is what we mean when we say a story held us in its spell. We are so deeply involved in the story we are unaware of anything else. Only the story.

Five senses? Yes, the five senses. And *all five* of them:

- sight
- hearing
- smell
- taste
- touch

Sight. Most of us understand the importance of descriptive words that help us see what things look like. We need one or two physical attributes to aid us in forming a picture in our minds. Think with me for a moment, and you will master the idea.

- What one physical characteristic do you imagine first when thinking of your mother?

- How about your best friend from childhood?

- Your most favorite pet?

- Your most obnoxious boss?

There is no need for long descriptions. In fact, sometimes that gets in the way of our own pictures. You don't make many pictures in your mind while you are watching television, do you? I thought not. That's because someone else has made all the pictures for you. Our imagination fills in what we don't know. If someone else has made the entire picture for us, there is no need for our imagination to make any pictures at all.

So give us those one or two details that will help us make a picture that will jump start our imagination. Tell us that the monster was big and green and ugly! That will definitely help me make a picture in my mind. But, don't stop there. Activate my other four senses as well. For maximum involvement in the story, I want to know what something big and green and ugly smells like, and what kind of sound it makes, and the texture of its fur. By the time you have told me about its hot breath on the back of my neck, that Thing will seem so real to me, you can scare me to death with your story. No matter how many special effects Hollywood develops, there is nothing scarier than our own imagination.

Hearing. Sounds can evoke strong emotion. Think about these auditory images.

- What sound says, "Welcome home"?

- What sound says, "You win"?

- What sound says, "Emergency"?

- What sound says, "You are loved"?

Often a sound gives us emotional context. Nothing says "anger" like the slamming of a door. Nothing says "boredom" like the slow ticking of a clock.

You can help us be in the setting of the story by mentioning the chirps of the crickets or the sounds of the songbirds in the trees. You can bring the story to life for us by speaking from the voices of the characters. You don't need to be the voiceover for an animated movie. Keep it simple. Just drop your voice a little when your grandfather is speaking in the story. Raise it a little when it is your grandmother who has the floor. The difference in pitch creates a distinction between the characters and helps us see the action in the story without becoming confused. It deepens our experience of the story and holds us in it. Sound effects like the creak of an opening door in a scary story or the plop of a drip of water can enliven the story for the listener.

But, remember, just as with sight words, less is more. Don't overdo it. You want any sound effects to complement the story, not compete with it. If you are good at sound effects, resist the temptation to make the story nothing but a showcase for your ability to make great sounds.

Smell. Odor is the strongest memory trigger. I got on the elevator at a downtown Dallas church and rode up to the top floor where the offices were located. When the doors opened, I was shocked to be getting off in front of their receptionist. I was so deeply present in my mother's kitchen of my early childhood, I had to shake myself a little to be in the here and now. I could see everything about that kitchen, down to the last crack in the linoleum, far more clearly than I had been able to visualize it in years. It took me a minute to realize that the overheated wiring in that old elevator smelled just like my mother's electric mixer. That smell had carried me back over six decades.

What odors do you associate with these experiences?

- A smell that says, "I'm in trouble!"

- A smell that says, "I have faith."

- A smell that says, "It's all over."

- A smell that says, "Easy street!"

Putting smells in our stories makes people more present to the story as it is being told and it helps people remember the story more once it is over. If you want the story to be truly memorable, try infusing it with smells. Doesn't have to be smells from the kitchen. It could be motor oil, or bleach, or typewriter ribbon, or hay. Doesn't have to be a pleasant smell, either. Could be gasoline, or garbage. Just help our noses be alive in the story, too.

Taste. Our sense of smell and our sense of taste are very closely linked. Mention gingerbread, and it is not just our sense of smell that comes to life. Our taste buds come to attention as well. Must be all that plumbing up there so close together. All those kitcheny smells mentioned above trigger our sense of taste as well as our sense of smell.

You don't have to lick something to know how it tastes. The smell of gasoline is so strong that when you smell it, you can taste it on your tongue. When you are near the ocean, you can smell it. It is also possible to taste it. You don't have to run down to the waves and stick your tongue in them to do so, do you?

Tastes can conjure up some powerful memories.

- A taste that says, "Grandma's kitchen."

- A taste that says, "Grade school lunchroom."

- A taste that says, "Dentist's office."

- A taste that says "Newly married."

There's lots of emotion in thinking about them, isn't there?

Give us tastes in the narrative that are appropriate for the story that is being shared. The mention of certain tastes can send us back into our own childhood. They can help us make a journey to a place we have never been. They can help us feel at home and comforted. Other tastes can make us feel uneasy immediately. Mention the taste of blood, and we feel your injury right away. Our response doesn't even wait for the details to unfold. We are already in the state of "red alert" because your words have created in us a sense of anxiety.

Touch. Wet or dry? Cold or hot? The skin is the largest organ of the body. Help bring our entire being into the story by giving us textural details with which our imagination can work.

Whether it is the comfort of much-washed flannel, or the stiffness and discomfort of a brand new uniform, give us the textures that will advance the emotion of the tale. Remember words imply more than is actually being said. If you are painting a picture of wealth, it says more to use words like "silk" and "cashmere" than it does to tell us that someone was rich.

- What touch says, "The weather is changing for the worse"?

- What touch says, "I feel your pain"?

- What touch says, "Poverty"?

- What touch says, "First love"?

 The longer the story is, the more important those sensory images become. They help to hold us in the story when the narrative becomes lengthy or complicated.

 Historical story really needs sensory imagery to hold the attention of your participants. You are taking them to a place that is different and hard to imagine. You may be fighting a sense of disinterest in the story because it seems like it is "educational" rather than entertaining. Spend the time to flesh out a full experience of the story that will include all of the five senses. That will enliven the story and create in the listener a sense that they were present as the story is unfolding. **This is true for sacred story,** as well.

I have a story from Texas history that I love to tell. It is fairly long.

I include some sensory imagery at the beginning to help set the listener in time and place. In the middle of the story I have built into the tale, "At lunch they stopped at a little place called Pecan Springs. There was nothing there but a stream of running water. But, that was all they needed. Pretty soon they built a fire and the whole area was filled with the smell of coffee and bacon."

There is no reason to include that information in the story. It does not advance the plot. The only reason I have placed it there is to activate the senses of my listeners, to heighten their involvement in the story at the midpoint, when their attention may have a tendency to lag. You will notice I have included two things everyone is familiar with that activate both the sense of smell and the sense of taste: coffee and bacon. Also, I have included two things that activate all five senses in a short period of time: fire and running water.

Each is very useful to include because they appeal to all five senses quickly. Fire has sight, sound, smell, taste and touch. So does a stream of running water. Placing either of them in a story at an appropriate place can be quite useful.

The more intense or emotional a story may be, the more important sensory imagery is to its success. The participant needs to be so deeply engrossed in the story that they can overcome our natural response to want to turn away when the going gets rough, and we begin to feel uncomfortable. Don't wait till you get to the difficult part to include sensory imagery. Weave it into the story from the beginning so they are too deeply involved in it to want to withdraw when you get to the hard parts.

Exercise. Choose one scene from your storyboard. Look at it and begin to imagine it as clearly as possible. In your imagination, turn it from a two-dimensional drawing into a three-dimensional scene. When you can see it clearly in your imagination, step into the scene and walk around in it. Don't just imagine what things look like. Experience the scene with all five of your senses. Take your time. Explore the entire scene. When you have experienced it as fully as you can, write down some of the sensory words or phrases that came to you. Don't take the time to write full sentences. On the picture you drew for that scene, jot down words and phrases you might want to use in your story. Continue this process with each of the scenes of the story.

LAYER FOUR

Characterization

**Tip: Get to know the characters in your story
intimately.
If you don't believe in them, no one else will.
You can't give away what you don't have.**

*"Whenever I dwell for any length of time on my own shortcomings,
they gradually begin to seem mild, harmless rather engaging little
things,not at all like the startling defects in other people's character."*
– Margaret Halsey

What do Elizabeth Bennett and Scarlett O'Hara have in common?
Captain Ahab and Atticus Finch? They may be fictional characters,
but they are completely believable and eternally memorable. No
matter what kind of story we are sharing, we would like it to be
peopled with characters that are **believable and memorable**.

If you are working with folktale or original material, you will
need to develop the character in your own imagination. If you are
using historical material, you may want to use your imagination
to fill in what you don't know based on what you do know. That
can be true of family or personal story, as well. You may have a
wonderful story that has been passed down in your family about
your great-grandmother. Just because she was your father's
grandmother doesn't mean you know much about what she
was really like. You probably never met her. You may not know
any more about her as a person than you know about Martha
Washington. Developing that family story becomes much like
developing a historical story, often with less research material
from which to draw.

We want to work to make the characters **believable** because:

- We want people to stay in the story and not get jerked out of it by a feeling of phoniness or false sentimentality.

- A participant who does not believe in the characters may withdraw their attention.

- A participant who does not believe in the characters will not make any emotional investment in the story and will not follow you into the deeper pool of the story.

In short, **if the characters are not believable, the whole story falls apart.**

We want to work to make the characters **memorable** because:

- It helps the listener or reader distinguish between the characters.

- It deepens the participant's experience.

- It creates a valuable memory.

To create a character that is both **believable and memorable**, we need a fully developed three- dimensional picture of this individual. Give us **one or two physical characteristics we can use to paint a picture in our imagination.**

But you don't want to stop with what someone looks like. Don't forget we have **five senses**. Try to activate as many of them as you can.

- What **sounds** do you associate with them?

- What **smells**? What **tastes**? What **textures**?

We want to truly know this character. Help us understand them.

Show us their **strengths**:

- not as a "laundry list" that sounds like the Boy Scout laws

- don't tell us, show us

But no one is all good. Show us their **shortcomings** as well:

- that doesn't make them less loveable or heroic, it makes them seem real

- it moves them from being "cardboard cut-outs" to being fully developed characters

What about **idiosyncrasies**?

An idiosyncrasy is neither a strength nor a shortcoming. It is a habit or action that is peculiar to an individual. Including idiosyncrasies:

- can help build a stronger picture of the character

- are more memorable than character traits

- are often endearing

Whenever my spring-loaded mother was forced by circumstance to sit still, she would occupy herself by pleating the end of her apron into tiny, precise pleats. When she reached the end of the fabric, she would snap it open and begin the process all over again.

Exercise. Use this character profile to flesh out at least two characters from your story.

One sympathetic one. One who is less appealing or approachable.

Building A Character Profile

"You can't write well with only the nice parts of your character, and only about nice things . . . I want to use everything, including hate and envy and lust and fear."
– Allison Lurie

What one physical characteristic will help us make a picture of this person in our imagination?

When you think of this character, what body part first comes to mind? Why?

What is something they often say?

Are they garrulous or taciturn by nature?

What's the mood projected in their communication? Are they loving? Resentful? Friendly? Gruff?

What kind of grammar do they use?

What kind of vocabulary? What does this tell us about them? What sounds do you associate with them?

What smell do you associate with them?

What are this character's strengths?

What are their weaknesses?

What are their idiosyncrasies?

What is this character's biggest fear?

What is their strongest allegiance?

What makes this character unique?

Point of View

**Tip: There are as many versions of a story
as there are people involved in the event.
Everyone sees it differently.
That means there are
an unlimited number of ways
you can choose to share it.**

*"Until the lion has his or her own storyteller,
the hunter will always have the best part of the story."– Chinua Achebe,
quoting an Ewe-Mina proverb*

Now it's time to consider who should be telling this story. From whose point of view can it most effectively be shared?

There are **two basic choices**:

- the omniscient narrator – speaks in the **third** person

- a character from the story – speaks in the **first** person

The omniscient narrator is often the voice of the story. That is particularly true in folktales. It is so common, in fact, that we hardly notice it at all. That can be both a strength and a weakness.

The **third-person** voice of the omniscient narrator:

- is easy to follow and comprehend

- knows and understands everything about the story and its characters

- tells the story without a personal agenda

- may seem wooden and emotionally detached

You can see this in the straightforward storytelling of Margaret Mitchell's *Gone With the Wind* and in *The Old Man and the Sea* from Ernest Hemingway or traditional fairytales such as *Hansel and Gretel* or *Rumpelstiltskin*.

The **first-person** voice may still be the narrator, but:

- may be harder for the participants to understand at first

- can only speak to what that character would know and understand

- has some agenda, often hidden

- offers the emotional immediacy of that character

- shares the story with the strengths and weakness of the character speaking

It is *Moby Dick*'s "Call me Ishmael." And it is *To Kill A Mockingbird*, given to us in the voice of nine-year-old "Scout."

In the novel *A Gathering of Old Men* by Ernest J. Gaines, we hear the story of the killing of a white man from more than a dozen elderly black men, each claiming to be the murderer. Each speaker tells the story with his own agenda. A profound picture of racism develops as the truth is revealed, hiding between the conflicting versions.

It is always tempting to use the main character to give voice to the story. This can be a strong and effective choice. The soldier in the foxhole knows the war intimately. Remember, however, that what he could share would be limited by his personal knowledge of war. His recounting of the story would also be influenced by any character flaws, like the desire to aggrandize his contribution, or his unwillingness to take responsibility for his actions.

The best choice, however, may be someone other than the main character. Choosing a supporting character as the "voice" of the story may give you a way to approach the main character with more depth and honesty. Author William Styron's novel *Sophie's Choice* is told more honestly from the point of view of Stingo than if it had been told in the voice of the secretive Sophie or Nathan the schizophrenic.

Choosing a "voice" to tell the story other than the omniscient narrator can give a fresh look at an old and well-known story. This is where adaptation of well-known stories comes into play.

One of my favorite storytelling festivals is the Oklahoma City Storytelling Festival, formerly called Winter Tales. At this event each year, the four featured storytellers agree that they will work up a version of a common story. On Saturday afternoon, everything else at the festival shuts down and everyone assembles to hear four separate versions of the same tale. It is called "Finding Your Voice." Each year brings delights and surprises. My favorite year was the year the commonly agreed upon story was *Cinderella*. Everybody knows that story. How could you possibly bring something new and fresh to the telling of that old tale so that contemporary listeners could hear it with new ears? Well:

- Don Doyle (www.don-doyle.com) from Arizona told it from the point of view of the Fairy Godmother's husband, the practical one who makes everything she does possible. It was whimsical and just plain charming.

- Onawumi Jean Moss (www.onawumi.com) of Massachusetts

told it from the point of view of the spirit of Cinderella's dead mother who had always been there looking out for her and "could not believe how that low-life woman was talking to her baby." Cinderella's mother had attitude!

• Angela Lloyd (www.angelalloyd.com) of California used the omniscient narrator's voice for her telling. The motivations were so human and so believable you never really understood exactly when her treatment became abusive. Isn't that the way life really is? If abuse happened all at once, we would recognize it and nip it in the bud. Instead it builds gradually. Angela's telling was about facing your own beauty and your own power.

• And David Novak (www.novateller.com) from North Carolina told a tale as much about the Prince as it was about Cinderella. It was about being challenged to come out from behind your mask, at the ball and in your everyday life. He used the omniscient narrator voice, but presented the story in iambic pentameter.

What a learning experience it was to hear those four versions of that time-worn tale.

Choosing to tell the story from the point of view of the antagonist or villain may be a source of humor. That is the case when the Big Bad Wolf gives his version of the story in Jon Scieszka and Lane Smith's picture book *The True Story of the Three Little Pigs*. It can also give a chilling or macabre opportunity to understand more about the dark side of human nature. Edgar Allen Poe's short story "The Tell-Tale Heart" gives us the chance to go on "a walking tour" through the mind of a murderer.
The decision about point of view is very important in historical story. If the omniscient narrator voice is used there is always the possibility that the story will end up sounding like a lecture.

Putting the story in the mouth of people in the story may be more appealing and give greater emotional impact.

Once you have made a choice of third vs. first person voice for the story, you will need to stick to that choice. Consistency is important if you wish to keep your participants in the story. When people get confused about who is speaking, they try to straighten it out in their minds. All the time spent doing this is time spent not listening. If the participant struggles to understand for very long, they will simply stop listening and withdraw.

If you want to bring understanding to any historical event, try telling it from more than one point of view. Multiple points of view allow for grappling with the forces that were at work when the event occurred. The voice of the omniscient narrator can know everything about the event and give a panoramic view of what occurred. But whether it is the Battle of the Greasy Grass or the Battle of the Little Big Horn depends on whether you include the voice of Sitting Bull or the voice of George Armstrong Custer. Perhaps the most effective sharing of it might be from the first-person point of view of warriors who fought with each of these famous leaders. This approach gives the opportunity for a more honest appraisal of how the personalities of the leaders shaped this event.

It is possible to move back and forth from third to first person as the story unfolds, but this must be handled adroitly to make it work. Great care must be taken to make sure the participant knows who is speaking in the story in order to avoid confusion.

Syd and Adrienne Lieberman (www.sydlieberman.com) have collaborated on a CD that takes us to the heart of the Civil War conflict. It is titled *Abraham and Isaac: Sacrifice at Gettysburg*. The Father Abraham in the title is, of course, Abraham Lincoln. The Isaac refers to Private Isaac Taylor. The narrative moves skillfully back and forth between third- and first-person voices. Most of the first-person narrative is from the journal of Private Taylor.

When we think of stories that need to be "heard with new ears," Bible stories come quickly to mind. The telling of these stories can be brought vividly to life in our imagination by the use of point of view. Barbara McBride-Smith (www.barbaramcbridesmith.com) brings unique renditions of biblical stories to life with charm and creativity.

People listening to **Bible stories** have often heard the story dozens of times over the years. There is a tendency to think, "Oh, I've known this story for years," then disengage from the listening process. All of the stories from the Bible are given in the third-person omniscient narrator voice. Choosing to tell the story from another point of view may be just what is needed to help the participants hear an old story with new ears. This:

- places us at the heart of the action

- gives the opportunity for a shift in perspective

- accesses the emotional core of the story

A commitment to accuracy in sharing the stories of the Bible or any other sacred text does not mean that you cannot use your imagination to fill in what we have not been told.

Exercise. Go back and look at your storyboard. Choose three characters from your story: two major, one supporting. Do a five-minute timed writing for each character of how each would see this story. For each of them, as soon as you begin writing, do not stop. Write for the five minutes on the timer. Once you begin writing from the point of view of each character, don't stop. Write continually. Don't block or censor what comes up. Whatever you write is right.

Emotion

**Tip: The human heart only opens from the inside
… and sometimes the hinges are rusty.**

*"Stories can conquer fear, you know.
They can make the heart bigger."*
– Ben Okri

People want to resonate with the emotion of a story as though
a tuning fork has just been struck within them. One of the chief
purposes of story of every kind is to give voice to human emotion.
If a story does not elicit emotion, no one is going to remember it or
think of it as noteworthy.

If the experience is to be successful for everyone involved, a
strong story requires careful tending to the emotions of:

- the characters in the story

- the people receiving the story

- the person presenting the story

Of Characters in the Story

Here's a place where you want to take extra pains to "show," not
"tell." Ask yourself which works better:

"I could tell he was really angry. He said, 'He'll be sorry.'" Or,

"He smashed his fist into the palm of his hand as he spoke.
'He'll be sorry.'"

Telling us how the character feels weakens the impact of the story. The person who receives the story does not have to do any thinking or feeling for themselves because the emotion involved has already been neatly labeled for them. They accept your pronouncement about what is happening and do not need to involve themselves at more than a superficial level.

"She was so scared." Or,

"She couldn't stop her hands from trembling, but she tried to pray."

"He liked her. She could tell." Or,

"He got a soft look on his face when she entered the room."

When we "show" instead of "tell," the listener activates their imagination. They make a clearer picture of what is unfolding in the story. They also give themselves permission to listen at a deeper level, a level that requires more of them emotionally.

Appeal to all five senses to help us feel the emotions of the characters in the story.
Remember all the things that were discussed in Layer Three about sensory imagery?
Your story will be strengthened if you go beyond telling us what things look like. Help us use all five of our senses so we feel as though we were there as the story is taking place.
Remind us of sounds, smells and textures that go with whatever emotion is being expressed.

Exercise. Examine your storyboard for places where the characters are feeling strong emotion. Identify the emotion: anger, joy, frustration. Whatever it may be, write the word that most accurately describes it on that scene. How will you "show, not tell" us? How will you convey those emotions?

Of Your Listeners

You cannot force people to participate. You can only invite them. People will only go as deeply into the story with you as they feel safe to do so. It is important to build a bond of trust with them. Think of yourself as the tour guide. You promise to take them on an interesting journey, and to bring them home safely.

Often the story breaks down because too much is asked of the listener too quickly. Gotta prepare them. There's no substitute for that.

I am often asked about the difference between storytelling and theater. One of the big differences is the care given to the listener by the storyteller. In a theater presentation, people sit in the dark and the play is presented with little or no thought to the emotions of the participant. Each is left to deal with the impact of the story alone. In fact, leaving the audience in shock is often the desired effect.

Thinking of yourself as a tour guide includes bringing the participants home safely emotionally. In the oral presentation of story, great care is given to the state of the listener. Because people move so deeply into story in their imaginations, it is important to make sure that they feel safe at the end of the presentation.

Stories come in all stripes and sizes, from original work to ancient epic. No matter what kind of story it may be, the thing we most need to know about it is, "What kind of response will people give to this story?"

There are four kinds of energy:

- HAHA
- AHA

- AHH
- AMEN

HAHA. Obviously, these stories make people laugh. From monstrously large tall tales to subtle sophisticated humor, these stories are for the body. When people laugh, they relax and let down their defenses. They build endorphins that boost the immune system and create a sense of physical well-being. These stories help build a sense of community and create a bond of trust between the teller and the listener.

There are many funny folktales from cultures all over the world. At heart, most of them deal with how silly human beings can be. It is easy to relate to these stories because all of us know people who behave like the characters in them. Literary stories from writers like James Thurber and Isaac Bashevis Singer may not be slap-your-knee funny, but are humorous because of the insight they give us into the human condition.

AHA. Like Kipling's *The Elephant's Child*, we are filled with "satiable curiosities." We are intellectually curious. We love to figure things out. AHA stories are for the mind. There is a huge range of material in this category.

Ghost stories
"Oh, I get it! That little girl that they saw at the top of the stairs, that's the little girl who died when the carriage turned over."

Stories of unexplained phenomena
What did fall from the sky in Aurora, Texas, in 1897, and what is buried in that grave?

Stories of unexpected endings
Such as the tales of Ambrose Bierce in *Occurrence at Owl Creek Bridge*

<u>Stories with riddles in them</u>, like those in *Clever Manka*
What is the sweetest thing in the world? (a good night's sleep)
What is the heaviest thing in the world? (a guilty conscience)
And what is the richest thing in the world? (the earth itself –
everything good for us comes from the earth)

<u>All those folktales from different cultures</u> that explain where
something comes from or why our world looks like it does (called
pourquoi stories – that's French for "Why?")
"Why the Sea Is Salt"
"Why the Sky Is Far Away"

AHH. These stories may be a little harder to describe, but you
know them when you hear them. These stories are for the heart.
Romances, legends, personal narrative, any story may fall into
this category. The story of your grandmother saving you from a
whipping when you were small. The story of Tristan and Isolde.
These stories remind us of what it means to be fully human.

If you have ever had the pleasure of hearing Donald Davis (www.
ddavisstoryteller.com) tell stories, you may remember the sound
his listeners made at the end of his story, a whole group of people
sighing together at the end of the narrative. With a large audience,
you can actually hear that outtake of breath. That's the sound of a
satisfied human heart.

AMEN. Uplifting and inspirational, these stories are for the
human spirit. They may be teaching tales from the world's great
religions.

Sufi tales from the collections of Idres Shah
The stories of the Bel Shem Tov
The parables of Jesus
Or original stories like those of Martin Bell in *The Way
of the Wolf*

Or *The Forgiveness Book* by Bob Libby and *Tales for the Telling* by William White

But, it could also be a story about your own faith journey or a spiritual experience you had recently at the supermarket.

The AMEN story helps us think about things that are larger than our tiny human lives. They help put us in touch with something sacred. Mostly they are short and give great closure.

It is a mistake to tell your listeners how to feel. By doing so you may short-circuit their deeper responses to your story. Leave them free to give whatever response is right for them. Often what people take from the story is quite different than what you take from it. Trust your listeners to take from it that which is real for them. Only a fable spells out the meaning of the story.

If you are crafting story, you will want to try to evoke as many of these responses from your participants as possible. I am always attempting to craft the perfect story, one that has elements of each of these forms of energy in it.

Exercise. Run through the plot that you have pictured for the story that you are crafting. Which of these forms of energy do you believe your listeners will give to the story?
What is its dominant mood? Do you want them to give more than one form of response? If so, in what ways can you help them give more diverse responses? Write the kind of energy you wish them to give (HAHA, AHA, AHH, AMEN) on the appropriate scenes of your storyboard.

Of Yourself

Sometimes what we want to share with others has a deep emotional significance for us. In some cases that is obvious. We are aware of it from the beginning. Other times, the reason we are attracted to a story may not be clear to us at first, but emerges over time. More often, over time deeper levels of meaning become clear to us as we continue to work with the material.

Perhaps the story you want to share is about your grandmother with whom you had a close relationship. When you begin to tell the story, you begin to cry. Of course you want to tell stories that move you. If they don't move you, why would you want to tell them? But if the story moves you to tears you cannot control, you need to stop because you are not ready to share it publicly yet.

As soon as you begin to tear up, your listeners are likely to stop listening. They move into caretaker mode: "Is he going to be all right?" "Someone should do something to help him." "Should I get him a glass of water?" "Should I hand him a tissue?" The listener's mind becomes full of chatter that makes it impossible to hear the story.

Ask yourself, "Am I in control of the story? Or is the story still controlling me?" Be honest with yourself. If the story is still controlling you, you aren't ready to tell it yet. No shame here. I have a folktale I have been working on for years that I still do not tell in public because it reduces me to tears.

How to Prepare to Tell an Emotional Story

Don't suppress those emotions. They are fuel for the journey. Use them wisely. If you suppress them, they will sabotage you later when you least expect it.

Journal about the experience and the feelings surrounding it.

Think of the story as "a work in progress."

Tell the story to a trusted pair of ears. Be careful in the selection of this first listener. Often those who are close to us are not capable of accepting the story or our creative process without becoming judgmental or acting on the desire to "fix" us.

Tell the story to that same pair of ears again – maybe several times if they will let you.

Continue to journal about the feelings that arise when you share it.

Begin telling it to small informal groups.

Share it in "work groups," such as writers' groups, storytelling guilds, open "mics" or story swaps. Look for places that by their nature are open to the idea of sharing a "work in progress."

Don't rule out getting some help from a pro if you come to see it is warranted.

This process is important because we want the stories we share to be art, not therapy. For a story to be art, we have to have processed our feelings surrounding the story so that we can guide the participants safely through the experience of the story. If we lose control, they are left high and dry to fend for themselves. Remember the tour guide analogy? As imaginary tour guides, we do not have the luxury of abandoning them somewhere along the journey. It is our responsibility to guide them through the landscape all the way to completion.

Susan Klein (www.susanklein.net) has said everyone must make a trip to the underworld. No one can do that for us. Making those painful journeys is a part of the price we pay for being human. When we return from the journey, we do not tell about it to make ourselves look heroic to others. Instead, we tell the story of our journey as a way of saying to others, "Look, I drew you a map. This might be useful to you on your journey. You're going to need a coin for the boatman. You will want to take some bread to throw to the three-headed dog. And safe travels, friend." We tell these tales to bless those who travel after us.

Exercise. Go back to your storyboard. Look at each picture in turn. Is there anything in this story that may make you feel overwhelmed or out of control? Be honest with yourself in your answer. If the answer is yes, make a plan working through your issues so that you are prepared to be a good tour guide throughout the story.

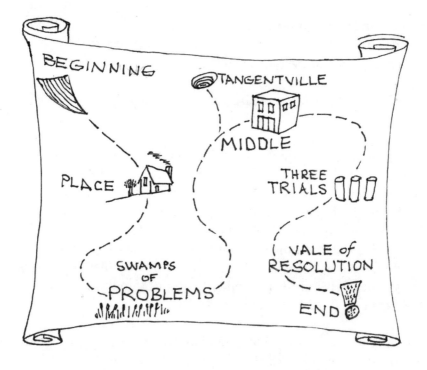

"That's what the true storyteller should be: a great guide, a clear mind, who can walk a silver line in hell or madness."
– Ben Okri

Connection

**Tip: Story is an antidote to
our greatest fear
– that we are alone.**

*"Storytelling reveals meaning
without committing the error of defining it."
– Hannah Arendt*

Train tracks run parallel to one another. No matter how long they continue, they never meet. We have all experienced stories like that. There was a story there, but the story and our lives did not intersect. We did not see ourselves or our lives in the story, so it did not make any connection with us.

To make a connection, the participants must see some link between the story and their lives. I am choosing the word "participants" here intentionally. Whether they are listeners or readers or watchers, if people do not feel any sense of participation in the story, no connection is being made.

Many of the elements we have already discussed can help people make a connection. Context, conflict, sensory imagery and emotion all play their part.

You may think that the subject of the story is what determines the amount of connection people feel. Well, of course, that too will be a factor. There are also ways of helping people make that connection whether they identify with the subject or not.

Two useful tools for helping to make that connection are:

- the rhetorical question

- the casual aside

Rhetorical Questions

Never ask children a rhetorical question. They will answer you. Out loud. Probably all at once.

Rhetorical questions can be very effective when working with teens or adults. When you ask a rhetorical question, an adult gives an answer in their mind. Forming the answer connects them more strongly to the story and causes them to listen with a deeper level of emotional commitment.

My friend Cathy Crowley once worked at Texas Women's University. When the university's birthday was being celebrated, she asked me to go with her to the celebration. That was not something I was keen on doing. She told me there would be good food and an open bar. I still was not very interested in going. There are not many people for whom I would put on a pair of pantyhose, but Cathy's name is on that very short list. So I gave in.

As soon as I entered the hotel ballroom and saw how the room was arranged, I thought, "Red alert! Red alert! Look at those chairs. Oh, no. There are going to be speeches."

Boy, am I glad I put on those pantyhose, for that is how I got to hear Dr. Beck Weathers tell the story of being left for dead on the side of Mount Everest. Now, I have to tell you that he was speaking to about 300 librarian types. There was not one person within the sound of his voice who had ever even remotely considered climbing Everest. In fact, our idea of roughing it was staying at Motel 6.

Dr. Weathers drew us right in from the beginning by using rhetorical questions to help us see the connections between his story and our lives with questions like:

"Did you ever want to do something? You wanted it badly. It was supremely important to you, but when you tried to explain it to other people you could tell they thought you were crazy? Remember that feeling?"

He had 300 bobblehead dolls in front of him. Every one of us was nodding because we had all experienced that. Why, I'd left a good steady job at a library to become a storyteller. The question he'd just asked was the story of my life. I remembered exactly what that was like.

At every twist and turn in his remarkable tale, Dr. Weathers helped us see ourselves in his story.

"Have you ever heard people talking about you when you weren't supposed to hear them?"

Of course we had. Being reminded of the experience in that way helped us identify with Dr. Weathers when he could hear people talking about him but was too deep in hypothermia to be able to respond.

Probably most of us had never experienced hypothermia, yet all of us had experienced having people talk about us. The rhetorical question connected us to his situation even though it was foreign to us. He found the piece of the experience that provided a "common denominator."

When he finished his presentation, people poured out into the hallway outside the ballroom. They were complaining bitterly about the temperature in the ballroom. They were stamping their feet and rubbing their hands together to get warm. They were upset that the hotel staff had let it get so cold in that ballroom. It wasn't particularly cold in that ballroom. All those people had been on Mount Everest for the last hour, freezing to death with Dr. Beck Weathers. That's the power of a well-crafted story.

Casual Asides

A casual aside is an offhand remark that seems to flow naturally from what was just being said. It does not elicit an actual internal answer from your participants, but it does resonate with them.

In one of my stories I usually say, "In those ancient days – the 1970s – children in Texas started to school decently and in good order, when children should start to school – after Labor Day. ("It's a plot, I tell you. The people who run the malls thought that up! If school starts in August you have to buy a hot weather wardrobe for your child. Eight weeks later you have to buy a cool weather wardrobe for them. By the time spring rolls around, do you think they can get their big toe in anything you bought in the fall? NO! You gotta buy another hot weather wardrobe for them. It's a plot, I tell you.") Then I return to the body of the story.

The more aware and in tune you are with your listeners, the easier it will become to have these remarks occur naturally. When you are dancing with a partner, after a time you begin to respond to their energy. Their response triggers a response from you. It is just like that. As you gain more experience you will find that you don't have to plan it or think it out ahead of time, it happens naturally. Storyteller Ed Stivender of Philadelphia uses casual asides masterfully to develop a closer relationship with his listeners.

Exercise. Think about the story you are crafting. What is the theme of the story? Write the theme or themes in two or three sentences. How is this theme mirrored in the lives of others? Write about that. How will you help your listeners make the connection between your story and their lives?

You can make connection with more than the theme. Examine your storyboard. Each place on it where you can see the possibility of making that connection, mark it with an X to represent an intersection – where things meet. Draw a circle around the X. That circle around the X makes a mandala, a sacred symbol. Whenever people recognize how much we have in common, that's sacred.

Humor

**Tip: If you think you aren't funny,
you just haven't found the kind of humor
that is a good fit for you.
Experiment.**

*"Humor is what happens when we're told the truth
quicker and more directly than we're used to."
– George Saunders*

Think of humor as being like the spice rack in the kitchen.
You would still eat regularly without using it, but it would be
pretty boring. Like spices in a recipe, adding humor can bring out
the energy in a story. Humor ranges from broad-based slapstick to
the most sophisticated.

It's always a good place to start. Laughter helps people relax. They
forget their worries for a little while and let go. Humor builds
trust in the storyer and encourages participants to take the journey
wherever the storyer leads. Time spent at the beginning building
that sense of trust is time well spent and will pay big dividends
later.

Humor is also important in helping participants deal with subjects
that may make them uncomfortable. Using humor in stories
that are intense or difficult keeps the participants from feeling
overwhelmed. It helps them stay connected even if the story goes
into dark and painful places.

Humor falls into two general categories:

- word play

- thought play

Word Play

Spoonerisms are the swapping of beginning sounds in two or more words so that "tons of soil" becomes "sons of toil." They are named for William Spooner who was afflicted with the unfortunate malady of doing this unintentionally – to the amusement of everyone but himself. There are entire stories based on this type of humor, "Rendercella and the Pransome Hince" is a good example.

Willy Claflin's stories told by his puppet companion Maynard Moose are filled with wordplay. I would put it in a category, but it is in a category all by itself. "The Mommy person was destreamly angriefied!"

Puns are funny because of their play on words. Alexander Pope's, "To err is human; to forgive, divine" becomes "To err is human; but it feels divine" at the hands of Mae West.

Puns may be embedded in the story for comic effect. They may also be the point to the entire story. If so, they are called **Shaggy Dog stories**. There is the long involved one about a mountain lion stealing a pair of new cowboy boots that belong to Roy Rogers. The entire story is a set up for the punch line "Pardon me Roy, is this the cat that chewed your new shoes?" sung to the tune of "The Chattanooga Choo Choo."

Banter is a teasing form of conversation in a good-natured manner. It is sometimes called **repartee**, an exchange of clever remarks. Think of it as sparring with words. It is the conversations in old movies with stars like Spencer Tracy and Katherine Hepburn.

You will find great examples in lots of romantic comedies.

Wisecracks are offhand comments about a situation or a person. Unlike banter, wisecracks are a one-way street. Carmen Agra Deedy (www.carmenagradeedy.com) tells zestfully funny stories that are filled with this type of humor.

Thought Play

Hyperbole is the comedy of exaggeration. It ranges from ramping up the situations in a story by a few degrees in order to get a laugh to the telling of full-scale, all-out tall-tale lies. Many effective personal stories utilize it, and it is the mainstay of the stories heard at a Liars Contest. Bil Lepp (www.leppstorytelling.com) is the undisputed master of this type of humor.

Irony is the use of words to say something other than what is meant. It is an expression of the incongruity between reality and the expected or hoped for result. Two things that depend on one another have become adversarial.

Mozart was deaf.

The best-known liar on the storytelling festival circuit is an ordained minister.

> "It took me three hours to figure out how to get to the help desk of my email carrier. When I finally reached them, they referred me to their Quick Links."

Sarcasm is a mocking form of humor. Sometimes it is bitter and intended to give pain. The word comes from the Greek and literally means "to tear flesh." It is the most common form of conversation on television situation comedies. It drives the songwriting of Randy Newman (www.randynewman.com). Many of the best bumper stickers depend on it.

"Be sincere, whether you mean it or not."

Looking at an object made by someone else:

"Is that supposed to be a frog?"
"Sure."
"From where, Chernobyl?"

Satire is also a mocking form of humor. Unlike sarcasm, its purpose is to expose wickedness or stupidity in the hope of creating change. "Saturday Night Live" skits are often based on this kind of humor.

Caricature is an easily recognizable representation of a person's or type of person's speech or mannerisms exaggerated to evoke laughter. Remember Chevy Chase being President Ford on "Saturday Night Live"? Andy Offutt Irwin (www.andyirwin.com) gives us Aunt Marguerite, the perfect caricature of an opinionated, elderly Southern woman.

Parody is a comic rendition of something well known that copies its style for humorous effect. Most "fractured fairy tales" are parody.

Willy Claflin's picture book *The Uglified Ducky* (www.willyclaflin.com) is fractured fairytale at its best.

I love to lead audiences in singing "The Overweight Hokey Pokey."

"You put your double chin in. You take your double chin out."

It is important to find humor that is a good fit for you and your personality. All humor is risky. Will they think it is funny? You have to put it out there and deal with their response … or lack of it. It is also important to make sure that the subject matter you choose is a good fit for both the audience and the venue.

Some kinds of humor are worth a second thought:

- blue humor

- dark humor

- inappropriate humor

Bawdy and blue humor has sexual or bathroom subject matter. It ranges from the crude to the highly sophisticated: fart stories from around the world or Vance Randolph's collection of scatological tales called Pissing in the Snow to classic erotic tales from *The Decameron* or *A Thousand and One Arabian Nights*. Folks who have the privacy afforded by reading are more accepting of this type of humor than those in live audiences.

You want the response to your story to be true enjoyment, not embarrassment and offense. So, you will want to choose the audiences for this type of material carefully. Some venues are both expecting and accepting of this material. In others, it would be a sure-fire way to make sure you would not be invited back. As the old folktale says, "Be bold. Be bold. But, not too bold." Remember, there is nothing more suggestive than the imagination."

Dark humor often deals with the bizarre, grotesque or violent parts of life. This is Detective Lenny Briscoe's habitual wisecracks at the beginning of the older episodes of the television show "Law and Order." It finds comedy in the subjects that most people would consider "unfunny." Some occupations, such as nursing and police work, lend themselves to this kind of humor. It is used as a kind of safety valve for those who have to deal with the traumatic every day. For most people it is an acquired taste. A little of it will go a long way. Overuse of it can make the storyteller seem callus and insensitive, turning people off.

> I called my brother who had taken my place for a few days at the bedside of our dying mother. I asked, "How's it going?" "Well," he responded, "if I could choose between coming back here or going back to Vietnam, I'd just as soon go back to Vietnam. At least you know who the enemy is, and you're allowed to shoot at them."

Inappropriate humor is called that for a reason. Nearly everything in life is funny if you spin it right. But, some things are never funny. Mostly that's humor at someone else's expense. Racist, and sexist humor is a sure-fire laugh killer for many people. Mean-spirited humor isn't funny, no matter what anybody says.

Timing

Many of us worry about boring people. We think if we talk fast enough that is less likely to happen. In fact, that choice moves us in the wrong direction.

Humor is as much about pauses as it is about language. For something to register as funny, the participants need time to make the picture in their imagination. If the delivery is too fast, there will be no picture – and if there's no image, there is no humor.

Once the humorous part has been delivered, give time for the responsive laughter. If we go on talking while folks are laughing, they squelch their response in order to hear what we are saying. They don't want to miss anything. Being hurried through a story makes people tense and less responsive.
You may be well served to:

- give a short pause before the humorous part to focus attention

- and to build anticipation

- give a long pause after the humorous part to allow
  for a full response

- begin again just before the laughter completely subsides

Exercise. What kind of humor do you use in daily conversation? That may be a good place to start. Look over the listing of types of humor given here. Ask yourself which of them appeals to you. Now, go back to your storyboard. Identify the places in your story where humor would be helpful. Mark each of those places with a stick-on flag. Think about which kind of humor would work in each of these parts of your story. Write the type of humor on the stick-on flag. Begin experimenting with the different types until you find what is comfortable for you and what works for the story.

Wisdom

**Tip: You can say anything in a story
– as long as you put it in
someone else's mouth.**

*"One can resist the invasion of an army,
but one cannot resist the invasion of ideas."*
– Victor Hugo

Each of us has an agenda. Because our personal agenda is shaped by gender, age, class, ethnicity, religion, politics and a host of other influences, we are often unaware of it. It influences the stories that we choose to share with our participants. It shapes the material with which we work. Storyteller and songwriter Bill Harley (www.billharley.com) is a Quaker. This commitment to nonviolence and social justice issues is a part of both the material which he chooses to share and the joyous way he shares it. If you didn't know this about Bill, you would not learn it from his endearing performances. If you did know this about him, you would see it in everything he does.

Working on a story, you may find you have something you want to say, some message you want to deliver. The story gives us opportunity to share with our participants the ideas and teachings that are important to us. That might be advice or social commentary. You may think this is corny, but story **is our chance to speak our truth**, however we see it.

This is the layer of story crafting I often refer to as "prophecy." Oh, I know the first thing you probably think of when I mention the word prophecy is the idea of foretelling the future. I guess that's the exotic part of being a prophet. Most everyone has heard of Nostradamus, even if they don't agree on what he predicted. I'm talking about the more common work of the prophet. The most common function of the prophet is to tell people what they may not necessarily want to hear.

Nearly every culture has some prototype of this exchange. In the African tradition, the griot is the history keeper and the conscience of the people. He remembers the tribe's history and stories, but one of his duties is to remind people of what they don't want to know. The storytelling of Baba Jamal Koram (www.babajamalkoram.com) is a natural extension of this tradition. In the Jewish tradition, the rabbi or the maggid often performs this function. The amazing legacy of Penninah Schram with *Stories One Generation Tells Another* and other work (www.sefaradrecords.com/artists.php?show=PeninnahSchram) shows that this tradition is still alive and thriving. Among Native American peoples, stories are often used to teach the people what they need to be reminded of. The clarity of the message in the stories of Dovie Thomason (www.doviethomason.com) is a part of this ongoing teaching process.

In Western European-based culture, we do not have such a clear cultural memory of this. The closest we have may be the jester's role in the court. It is the job of the jester to make the king laugh. Sometimes, however, it is also the role of the jester to tell the king the truth, whether he wishes to hear it or not.

As the storyteller, you have the bully pulpit. However, **having the bully pulpit does not give us the right to bully people.** As with every other aspect of storying, you want to weave any message you wish to deliver into the story in an artistically pleasing and effective manner. That process is what Chicago-based storyteller Susan O'Halloran (www.susanohalloran.com) calls "teaching without preaching" in her honest and important work with diversity.

A literary story is the creation of one individual. It contains the wisdom and the insight of the individual that created it. There are many beautiful literary stories that are worthy of being told. For better or worse, they are limited by the consciousness of the writer.

Rudyard Kipling's "How the Camel Got His Hump" from *The Just So Stories* gives us Kipling's thoughts on the power of words to create our reality, but in an amusing manner. Unfortunately, his work is flawed by his belief in colonialism.

The folktale is the product of an entire culture, the culture from which the story springs. Folktales contain the accumulated wisdom of humankind. In the folktale there are often important life lessons about ways of living in our world. They are filled with messages about the importance of family, and how to treat others. In the folktale, the virtues of honesty, loyalty, cooperation, compassion and humility are modeled for the listener. From time out of mind the older generation has used these stories to teach the younger generation how to live in harmony, how to live successfully in the culture.

When I tell a Scottish folktale called "The Woman Who Flummoxed the Fairies," I come to a part of the tale where the husband finds himself falling. He lands in fairyland where everything seems strange and threatening to him.

I tell this story to children knowing they receive a lot of messages from television that stress the importance of physical beauty. I always take a moment in the story to help them think about what a lasting relationship is really based on. I say something like,

> "He landed with a plunk in fairyland. He jumped up, angry and confused. But he stopped short, for there was his wife. One of the reasons he married her was because he knew he

could trust her. Just the sight of her made him feel calmer. He said, 'I'm glad to see you. There's strength in being together.' And he waited to see what was going to happen next."

It only takes a moment to plant a
seed/thought
that might grow in the future.

The playwright and National Public Radio commentator Kevin Kling (www.kevinkling.com) is best known for his personal narratives. Recently I heard him tell a folktale. It had this amazing moment in it.

> "Jack was walking through the village. He passed by Death's house … because Death always lives in the heart of the village."

It may seem like such a small thing. But, in our scared-to-death-of-death culture, it is a kindness to remind people that Death is always nearby and a natural part of our lives.

Heather Forrest (www.heatherforest.com) is a storyteller who is highly skilled at pointing out potential life lessons in the folktales of the world. Her book *Wisdom Tales From Around the World* is a great resource.

"And the moral of the story is…." Oh, please! Our participants are intelligent people, capable of thinking for themselves. We don't want to beat people over the head with the message. If we do our work effectively, they will get it. When it is handled clumsily, it actually distances people from what we wish to teach them.
Only a fable has an obviously stated moral. Leave those to Aesop:

"Slow and steady wins the race."

Historical story gives us much opportunity to comment on social ills, both large and small. Racism and sexism are often the central themes in these stories. Even when that is not the case, there is the chance for social commentary on the timelessness of things such as greed and stupidity or the misuse of power. It is often easier for people to learn from the ills of another time than from those of their own. Award-winning Choctaw author and storyteller Tim Tingle (www.timtingle.com) often creates stories around historical events. *Walking the Choctaw Road* contains a moving and miraculous story called "Crossing Bok Chitto." In the oral telling of the story, Tim says, "And Martha Tom decided to do something she had never done before. She decided to trust someone of another color." Would that that thought would take root in all our participants.

Sharing sacred story from any tradition has at its heart the agenda of helping people connect to the life of the Spirit. These stories have great power and should be handled carefully. Japanese-American storyteller Motoko (www.motoko.folktales.net) thoughtfully and beautifully introduces us to teaching stories from the Buddhist tradition.

It is easy to get carried away and cross the line between "teaching without preaching" and proselytizing. This is a situation where sensitivity to the beliefs of others should guide us. **We are creating art, not planning a tent revival.**

I tell a set of stories called "Wading In the Jordan" about being with my mother and her sisters during the time when they are aging and transitioning into death. Because it is episodic, I made the choice to stitch it together with a hymn. I wanted to represent my mother honestly, but many of her favorite songs were very heavy on "Power in the Blood." Because I knew that many of my participants would be from religious traditions that were different from my mother's, I spent a lot of time choosing the hymn. I did not want references in the hymn to pull people out of the story. I finally settled on the chorus of "Bye and Bye I'm Gonna See the King" by Blind Willie Johnson. It represents my mother's faith fairly and pulls people deeper into the story.

Exercise. Is there some bit of advice you want to offer your participants? Would it work well as a rhetorical question or as a casual aside? Or would it be a more useful choice to put the idea in the mouth of one of the characters in the story? If so, which one would be the most believable choice? Go to your storyboard and mark the place or places in the story where you will place these ideas with the letter P. If when you are finished there are so many flags on the pages that it looks like a cemetery on Memorial Day, back up.

What can you learn from this?

Word Choice

Tip: Learn every new word you encounter. Your
Vocabulary
is your toolbox.

*"The difference between the almost right word and the right word
is really a large matter – it's the difference between
the lightning bug and the lightning."*
– Samuel Clemens as Mark Twain

Effective narrative is the result of a million times a million tiny
choices. **Each word chosen has an effect.** It gives shape and form
to the narrative. Your choice of the form of speech (i.e.: noun,
adverb, etc.) transmits mood and emotional coloration. Often the
arrangement of phrases within a single sentence affects the order
in which the audience receives clues. Choose carefully. Every
word utilized should be a conscious choice.

Use Precise Language

Make every attempt to say as close to what you really mean as
possible. Careful choice of language will increase your chances of
creating an effective work. Sometimes, a thesaurus is handy when
toying with words. Occasionally, just listening to the cadence
of how you feel a given character would speak will result in
surprising and satisfying word choices.

Think of the difference created by the use of these words, which
mean basically the same thing.

Read each of them aloud and savor the word as you say it.

odor

        scent

fragrance

         stench

whiff

            aroma

  stink

     reek

Although each means essentially the same thing, each has a different feel to it and conjures up a different response within us. Each paints a different picture.

The use of just one word over another can radically alter the image in the mind of the participants. Try reading these two sentences aloud:

He would always remember the fragrance of her perfume.

He would always remember the stench of her perfume.

Quite a different image, right?

Be Specific, Not General

Help your participants by giving them the most exact information possible. Communicate clearly. Leave as little room as possible for being misunderstood.

<u>She was upset.</u>
This is too general. It does not give us enough information or tell us how we should respond emotionally. We are not sure if we should be avoiding her or comforting her.

<u>She was furious.</u>
This is very specific language. It is strong and direct. There is no doubt in our mind how she is feeling or how we should respond. As soon as we read this sentence, we are ready to go into duck-and-cover mode. We are waiting for the explosion that we know is eminent.

Be Eloquent

Use all the scope of your vocabulary to entice us into making a commitment to the story, both intellectually and emotionally. Remember, being eloquent does not mean being verbose. In fact, the more eloquent your use of language, the fewer words you will need to get the same effect.

Storyteller Janice del Negro's work is infused with beautiful use of language. The elegance and precision of her words sets her work apart. She often says, "Revision is where you get to show that you are brilliant." She's right.

In general, you will want to avoid:

- slang

- clichés

- platitudes

Slang is casual and nonstandard language. Because it is jargon, you run the risk of having some people misunderstand what you mean. Because it changes quickly, using it makes it easy to sound dated. You want more enticing language.

Clichés are hackneyed, tired and worn out. People tend to be deaf to them because of overuse. You want to give them something fresh and new to experience.

Platitudes are insipid and trite. They short-circuit any real experience of the story because they bore people. Whether it's laughter or tears, you want to go deeper.

Choose Language That Is a Good Fit for the Story

An ancient epic or old fairy tale calls for language with a sense of timelessness about it. Nothing can throw the participants out of an old story as quickly as the use of modern slang in it. Even a word or two of contemporary slang can throw your participants out of the story and make it difficult for them to regain their sense of wonder even when they regain their place in the tale.

The mood you are creating with some stories will lend itself to stately, formal language. Colloquialisms and folk expressions work well for the telling of folk tales and tall tales. Romantic stories can be filled with words and images that evoke emotion.

Beware of Using Labels

There is an attraction to doing so because it seems a clear and simple way to communicate with your participants. They are clichés. Also, what seems like a time saver may turn out to be a detriment. Every time you label a person or group in a story, you run the risk of offending all those who would have used that label to describe themselves.

I tell a story about a wedding. I want to "show, not tell" how different the two families are. If I attached labels to each family (conservative or liberal, Republican or Democrat), I would be telling, not showing. I would also run the risk of insulting some or all of my listeners. Instead, I choose to show the differences between the two families.

My intern Gene walked out to the parking lot with me to carry some boxes. Standing in the middle of the parking lot, he said, "Have you noticed how you can tell whether the cars are from the bride's side or the groom's side?"

I said, "I guess you can tell by which cars cost more."

"Well, maybe," he said. "But you can sure tell a lot by looking at the bumper stickers." He was right.

> Charlton Heston Is My President. *That would be the bride's side.*
> Starfleet Academy. *Groom's side.*
> You can have my gun when you pry my cold dead fingers off of it. *Bride's side.*
> Protect the right to arm bears. *Groom's side.*
> Go to church this Sunday. *Bride's side.*
> My karma ran over my dogma. *Groom's side.*

Labels may be easy to use, but they won't get you any laughs.

Exercise. The use of language is skill based. We learn skills best by practicing them. Choose a four-hour block of time to practice using precise and elegant language. During that period of time, you will think before you speak and practice being eloquent. Avoid:

- slang
- clichés
- platitudes

Choose to say everything with fresh, new wording and expression.

When you revert to old language habits, don't beat yourself up. Just acknowledge the way you spoke and recommit to the process for the remainder of the four hours.

At first you may find this difficult. If, however, you will persist in doing it on a regular basis you will develop the habit of eloquence. (It takes 21 days to create a new habit.) It will have transfer value to everything you do.

Putting It All Together

You have spent some time putting the basic plot through **ten different layers of narrative enrichment**. I imagine you have learned a lot about your story and how you want to share it with others. Let's begin putting it all together.

Go back to your storyboard. Think through the story from beginning to end. Decide exactly where you want to begin the story. **Try arranging the pictures of your storyboard in differing orders.** Do you want to present the story in chronological order? Or will some other arrangement of the sequence of events serve your participants better?

There are some basic questions to ask yourself about how the story will be developed.

• Do you want the story to begin with context – scene setting?

• Would you prefer to start with **strong characterization?**

• **Or would the introduction** of the conflict be the place to begin?

There are strengths to each of these possibilities.

Beginning with context gives the participants **a deep understanding of the situation** before the conflict is introduced. If the context is important, this may be the best choice. Most of Robert Morgan's novels are written in this manner. *Gap Creek* is an excellent example.

Introducing the characters first offers the participants the opportunity to **care deeply** about them before the pace of the narrative picks up speed. It may make their behavior more understandable later in the story. Howard Norman's *The Bird Artist* gives us strong characters we care enough about to follow them throughout the narrative.

Conflict is an **immediate attention gatherer**. Most "action" films are formatted this way. Native American author Susan Power's *The Grass Dancer* begins with conflict that is both gripping and poetic.

Wherever you decide to begin the story, know that **the beginning of the story is much like the entrance to a home**. You want it to be attractive to those who come to visit. You want them to be encouraged to come inside and visit. You want the story to have some "curb appeal." So give some thought to where you want to begin in order to entice your participants to linger with you for a while.

Once you have chosen a sequence for the shaping of the story, **examine the picture you chose to be first in your storyboard**. Look it over carefully. **Note all the stick-on flags** from each of the layers that were discussed. Do you see places where you decided your participants would need **context** in order to understand the story? In what way do you feel you can best accomplish that? If need be, go back to the narrative layer concerned and reread what was discussed.

Look for the flags you used to indicate the potential for **conflict** in the story. Did you mark them with an E for external, or an I for internal? Conflict is going to build the tension in the story and give it substance.

One by one, go back through the narrative layers, reviewing what you want to include in the first part of the story. They will serve as a strong reminder of what you want to include in the beginning of the story. **Examine all the other symbols, words and phrases** that you wrote on that portion of the storyboard. Each of them represents a clear idea you had about what you wanted to include or how you wanted to include it.

Now we've actually come to the point where you are going to begin to write.

I bet you thought this time was never going to come! Sometimes it feels that way. But, all the pre-writing that you have done will make the writing process so different than if you had bypassed it all and started by sitting down at the computer.

However you have arranged them, write from each of the pictures in turn until you have completed the process. If you get stuck for a moment, go back to the discussion of that layer of narrative and think through what you need. You will work it out. Be patient. This process supports your creative and elegant completion of the entire project.

Sharing It Aloud

**Tip: When your work is shared aloud,
participants only get one chance to understand it.
There is no "instant replay." It must be
clear to your listeners immediately.**

You may be thinking that this section has nothing to do with you. Hold on a minute! No matter what type of storyer you may be – writer, filmmaker, poet – there are going to be times when you will want to share your work orally. Maybe you'll be asked to read from your work. Perhaps you'll have a chance to make a presentation about it to someone important – like someone who might publish it or produce it. When that time comes, you will want to do it as effectively as possible. So, stick with me.

I have been to poetry readings and writer's groups where I would not be able to identify the presenters in a police lineup an hour after the event was over. Oh, I could probably identify the tops of their heads. But, their faces? Nope. Never saw them. They stared at the paper through the entire presentation. This is a very inefficient way to share your work. You want to give your work the possibility of reaching people. That means you want to deliver it in a way that gives it a chance to shine.

One person stands in front of a group of people and holds them breathless with just their voice. That's the power of storytelling. It has been a method for impacting people from time out of mind. It only makes sense to look at the skills used by storytellers and apply them when you share your own work. Before we discuss some of those skills, remember that sharing your material orally is a different experience for people than if they were reading, or sitting through a media presentation. **You may need to make**

a few simple changes to help the participants understand and appreciate what you have created.

When people are reading, if they become confused, they drop back a few paragraphs and re-read the passage until they understand it. If they are greatly confused, they can go back to important passages and reacquaint themselves with facts or characters that were introduced earlier. If they are reading poetry, they can study a phrase over and over until they have the sense of it and find the beauty in it. They cannot do any of these things when they are in a group of people listening. Listening, they only have one chance to understand it. There is no "instant replay." That single fact accounts for most of the changes that you may want to make when you share your material orally.

Here are a few things to consider in preparing for being in front of a living, breathing audience, no matter what size.

- If it is important, find a way to tell it to them twice.

- Use more nouns and fewer pronouns.

- Remind them of what you shared earlier.

When you are seated in an audience and the person speaking mentions something, let's say a sled, your automatic response is to begin to think about what you know about sleds. In a moment, those thoughts run from the general to the personal. Your internal dialogue may sound something like this. "I used to have a sled. It was a great sled. Wooden with red handles. Sledding was really fun. I wonder what ever happened to that sled. Last time I remember seeing it was in my parents' garage. I bet my sister has that sled!"

It isn't that you weren't interested in what the presenter was saying. This is just the way the human mind works. We go off on little internal trips every day in this way. All the time you are in your head following that internal dialogue, the presenter is still talking. You have missed some of what was being said. I am sure you have experienced this many times. It is a natural process. The folks who are listening to you when you are presenting will be doing the same thing. So, if there are things that are really important to the understanding of the material, find an artistic way to tell it to them twice. That increases the possibility that they will grasp it.

When we don't understand what the presenter is talking about, we may spend a little time trying to puzzle it out. If we continue to be confused, the most likely response is that we will withdraw emotionally and begin to think about something else. Telling something important to the participants twice increases the possibility that they will understand the needed information and be less likely to withdraw their attention because they are confused.

Of course you will want to do this in a skillful manner.

vary the wording
or
change your tone of voice

When telling historical stories, I often give needed factual information in the form of dialogue, as we discussed in the layer about context. It is easy to have one of the characters repeat what the other character has said, using different wording.

"The Married Women's Property Act now gives married women the right to own property in their own names. This is the first law that gives women any legal rights," Lucy said.

Elizabeth asked, "So this law allows ladies to control their own property if they are married? But does it apply to unmarried women?"

"No, dear. They are still controlled by fathers or brothers. That fight is still to come."

In many of my personal experience stories, I use the technique of repeating what I have said by changing my tone of voice.

"You want me to come to the morgue to look at a body?" I asked into the phone. And to myself I whispered, "Identify a body?"

When you are listening, **the use of pronouns can be a source of confusion**. He did this. He did that. He did this. Then he did that. Before long the listener doesn't know to which "he" you are referring. Was it the father who got angry and slammed out the door? Or the son? With so many "he's" flying through the air, it is difficult to tell. To help the participants keep their place in material that is shared orally, use proper names far more often than you would in material they would be reading.

Another technique that is quite useful in an oral presentation is to reintroduce any character that has not appeared in the story in awhile. **Remind them of what you shared earlier**. A character re-enters the story near the end of the material. No mention has been made of him for several minutes. The listeners have heard a lot of things since they last heard of him. It can be useful to your listeners to be reminded of who he is and what his relationship is to the other characters in the story.

"She looked up and noticed Charles hastening down the street. She thought to herself, "I'm so
glad my sister married him.""

The line could just as easily be, "She looked up and noticed her brother-in-law, Charles, hastening down the street. She thought to herself, "I wish my sister had never laid eyes on that man."

Remember, when you are sharing your work aloud, just a few small changes in your material will make it **easier for participants to follow.** You want to hold them in the material. Everything you can do to make this easy for them will pay big dividends. When they can follow the material, they can give themselves over to being truly moved by it.

The Storyteller's Art

Storytellers have been holding people spellbound since we all lived in caves. One person stands in front of a group of people, young or old, and holds them in the palm of his hand with nothing but his voice, his eyes, his gestures ... and, of course, his story.

It is a venerable art form, but it is still being utilized every day. Every time you tell someone about something that happened when they were not physically present, you are telling them a story.

It has a beginning, a middle and an end. In fact, it has all the elements that we have been examining in this book. You tell stories every day. You have been doing so since you discovered that you have the gift of language. All the skills that you have used in sharing your stories everyday in conversation **are the same skills you will put to use to share your story aloud in a more formal setting:**

- know the material

- acknowledge that the listeners are co-creators

- use your voice effectively

- make good eye contact

- let your body help tell the tale

- keep them in the story

- pace yourself and your telling

- face your fears

One of the questions I am most often asked is, "How can you remember all that?" People seem particularly afraid that they will forget the story if they try to tell it. Many people write the story out, then memorize what they have written word for word. Then they tell it exactly the way they memorized it. There are a couple of potential problems with that method. One is when you have memorized something, if you forget a piece of it, you may find it impossible to go on with the story. Think of all that poetry you learned in high school. As soon as you came to a word you could not remember, you were shot down in flames. Memorizing a story works the same way.

I don't memorize the words in the stories. Over the years I have found what is for me a much more effective method. Instead of memorizing the words, I memorize the pictures.

If you have been following the exercises set out in this book, you will already have made a set of pictures for the scenes in your story. If you haven't done so, it's not too late. Make your storyboard now.

Go back to your storyboard and look at the pictures in sequential order. If you will **learn the order in which the pictures occur**, telling the story can then be as simple as describing what is happening in each of the pictures in their turn. If I tell you what is happening in the first picture, the second picture, etc., by the time I share what is happening in the last picture, I have told you the basic story. Maybe I won't remember the lovely words I was going to use to describe her dress, but I won't be standing there, sucking air, trying to remember what comes next. **What comes next can be as simple as describing what happens in the next picture.**

In my storytelling sessions, I am usually smart enough to remember not to ask young children if they have questions. Usually if you do that, every hand goes up. But there aren't really any questions; everyone wants to tell you about their dog. However, once I forgot and asked if any of the kindergarteners had questions. A hand flew up immediately. A little guy asked, "Do you memorize those stories?" Before I could respond, the boy next to him jabbed him with his elbow and answered, "No, stupid. She knows them by heart!"

I wasn't impressed with the violence done to his classmate, but I was really impressed with his answer. He was absolutely right. I don't memorize them. And I do know them by heart. It was amazing to me that he understood there is a difference.

You want to know your story by heart. You want to know what happens in the story so well that it is a part of you. Knowing the story well will do a great deal to increase your confidence. That's important.

When it is time to share your story, things are likely to happen that you didn't anticipate. Someone's cell phone will ring in the middle of the story. An oblivious waiter may begin clattering dishes. If you are telling outside, you may have any number of things to deal with, from weather to bugs. You want to know your story so well that you can go on with the telling no matter what is happening around you. We live in a culture where folks are used to being at home watching television. When they get engrossed in the story, they forget where they are and that the storyteller can see them. In a way, I guess that is a compliment. You want to know your story so well that when you look out and see an audience member picking their nose or scratching something you'd rather not know about, you'll be able to proceed without a hitch. You may be thinking right now that I am only referring to children in the audience. Believe me, I am not!

When you share your story aloud, it is important to remember that although you may have created the story, **the listeners are co-creating it in their imagination as it is unfolding.** Here is what often happens: you begin to tell your story. The listeners are dwelling on the first scene, creating it in depth in their minds. You have already sped on to scene two. They have to abandon their involvement with scene one in order to catch up with you. And, before they have really had a chance to experience scene two, you are half way through scene three. Telling at this pace gives the listeners little opportunity to participate in the experience. It is frustrating to the listener for you to tell so quickly that they do not have time to make the pictures or savor the sensory imagery.

Acknowledge their role to yourself and do everything you can to make that co-creation an easy process. **Pace the telling of the story to match their ability to create the pictures in their minds.** If they were reading, they could choose their own pace. This mutual creation process, however, relies on your ability to present the material at a digestible rate. Slow down. Don't try to force feed them. It doesn't work.

The human voice is a powerful tool for helping the participants enter the world of the story. For maximum benefit, it must be used effectively.

Speak loud enough to be heard. If they can't hear you, they can't enjoy the story. Be aware of dropping your voice too low at the end of words or sentences. Knowing whether you said "Canon camera" or "Candid Camera" can make a lot of difference in their ability to understand the material.

Vary your tone of voice. Use an expressive voice that helps communicate the emotion in the story. Not phony and over the top, but a heightened sense of feeling.

In general:

- Happy sounds fast and soft

- Angry sounds fast and loud

- Sad sounds slow and soft

- Confused sounds slow and loud

Try watching some reruns of the television show "M.A.S.H." Listen to the sounds of the actors' voices. You will hear the whole gamut of human emotions being expressed if you pay careful attention.

If you wish, you can create a different voice for every character in the story. It isn't necessary, but it can be fun. Andy Offut Irwin makes great use of the voice he has created when he tells stories from the point of view of Aunt Marguerite (www.andyirwin.com). Remember, if you do make voices for the different characters, you will need to keep them straight. You'll have to use the same voice for the same character throughout the story or confusion will reign supreme.

You want to make eye contact with everyone in the group. The back row. The front. The folks seated on the sides. Don't leave anyone out.

Often when we are nervous, we realize that we have been moving our eyes back and forth as though we were security cameras scanning at the bank. This isn't really eye contact.

The word "contact" means I looked at you long enough for you to register that you were being looked at.

When we become aware that this scanning process has been taking place, what it usually indicates is that we have also been talking too fast.

Take a deep breath. Relax. Begin speaking at a slower rate of speed. **Address a phrase to a single pair of eyes** toward the back. Move your focus and address the next phrase to someone near the front. Speak a phrase directly to a set of eyes on one side of the group, followed by one to a set on the other side. Now work the center of the group. By breaking what you are saying down into phrases, you will be telling at a reduced speed that will give the listeners a better chance to participate in the story. You will also be making much stronger eye contact with your listeners. You will probably have calmed yourself in the process.

We can't force people to listen to our stories. We can only invite them into the experience. If we stand with our hands on our hips in "fight or flight" position, it makes the listener uncomfortable. Watching someone with their arms folded across their chest is off-putting.

Use your body language to invite people into the story.

Assume a relaxed pose, and help people feel that you are glad they are there to listen.

Many of us talk with our hands. In fact, some of us would be hard-pressed to talk without them. **Constant gestures are bewildering**. If you use gesture more sparingly, the gestures you do use will receive more attention. Use them to help propel the action of the narrative, as though you are observing things in the story as they are taking place.

> "The old man saw his son coming a long way off." (Arm outstretched and pointing as though watching the boy's approach.)

Moving a step or two, or turning your head from one side to the other can be an efficient way of helping people understand who is speaking in the story. Larger movement from one place to another can help indicate a transition for one part of the story to another. When using these movements, be careful not to lose eye contact with your listeners in the process.

Some storytellers are more physical in their telling than others. Storytellers like myself, who use a conversational style, often use little movement. Jim May (www.jimmaystoryteller.com) uses gesture only sparingly. That minimalist approach is a good fit for his Midwestern style. Milbre Burch's work is filled with natural and meaningful movement (www.kindcrone.com).

Japanese-American storyteller Motoko (www.motoko.folktales. net) carefully crafts her movements to create the characters, as well as carry forward the narrative. Her attention to detail in her movements creates a seamless story.

How much movement will you want to use in your storytelling? That's something you will need to experiment with until you find the style that works for you. You will want it to be a good fit for your personality, so that it feels natural and doesn't make you self-conscious.

Throughout the pre-writing material that was presented in this book we have talked about the importance of keeping people in the story. We don't want anything in the story that is going to jerk them out of the tale. The same thing is true for the presentation of the story, as well.

We don't want to do anything that will distract people and keep them from listening.

- stand still; don't fidget

- avoid playing with your jewelry or your clothing

- help folks focus on the story

It's not about you. It's about the story. Give it center stage. Be careful not to do anything that will compete with the narrative as it unfolds.

When we are nervous or excited, it is easy to begin the story at an intense pace. When we do that, we often reach the part of the story where we should be building the suspense, only to find we cannot increase the intensity at the needed part because we have been it telling that way from the beginning of the story. How can we "ramp it up" when we have been at full throttle from the start? **Pace yourself**. Begin at an energetic pace, but give yourself room to increase the energy in the story, as it is needed.

I have also seen people use so much energy at the beginning of the story they had nothing left by the time the ending occurred. The story fell flat because the teller exhausted herself and could not deliver the ending effectively. The energy needed to share a story looks like a bell curve. Save enough spirit to give the tale its dynamite ending.

Let's think together for a moment about stage fright, OK? You are familiar with the symptoms: sweaty palms, shortness of breath, feeling cold and clammy or downright nauseous. Everyone has felt that way at some point. Anyone who says they have never experienced it is probably lying. Even seasoned storytellers have to deal with it.

Current advice about the jitters usually includes imagining the people in the front row in their underwear. I guess that is supposed to help us relax. My imagination, however, is so vivid I find the idea distracting, even provocative, if the right people are present.

What can you do when you are overcome with stage fright?

I really do have a suggestion, but first I want to make the point that the best time to deal with stage fright is long before it happens. **Knowledge** is often the antidote.

- **know your story well so you won't feel unprepared**

- **learn as much about the event as possible so you are comfortable**

That kind of knowledge can build confidence. But, you can be well-prepared and still experience a bout of white-knuckled terror. **What then?**

- **breathe**

Fear is excitement without breath. When we get frightened, we begin to restrict our breathing. We begin ragged, shallow breaths from the back of our throats. That actually increases our experience of fear. Stop and breathe. Focus on your breathing. Breathe in as deeply as you can. Breathe from your solar plexus. Try to fill your entire being.

Explore the different kinds of breathing exercises that others have used effectively. You will find them in books for singers and actors. Developing a routine of breathing   that you use every day will give you a foundation to draw on when stage fright or performance anxiety rears its ugly head.

Enthusiasm can be thought of as the opposite of fear. The word comes from two Greek words, "en" and "theos." Its original meaning was to be filled with the breath of the Divine. So breathe. Fill yourself up with the breath of the Divine, whatever that means for you. Being filled with the breath of the Divine leaves no room for fear. Stage fright will dissolve naturally, leaving you with calmness and confidence.
Henry David Thoreau told us, "The only way out is through." Don't let stage fright keep you silent. Every teller has experienced it. None of them ever died from it! Acknowledge your feelings and move forward. Trust your stories. Trust your listeners. Most of all, trust yourself. You are up to this challenge. So, go out there and tell.

Just don't forget to breathe.

Index